Praise For *Labor Power and Strategy*

"In Our Revolution we shout, 'When We Organize, We Win,' but organize who and win what? *Labor Power and Strategy* is a great collection of Womack and ten organizers debating strategic workplace organizing versus associational or more general organizing at workplaces or in communities. Womack, in a long initial interview and in the conclusion, argues that without organizing workplace choke points, we are left with the spontaneous movements that come and go. Several of the ten organizers essentially argue that the spontaneous can become conscious and long-lasting. Grab the book and take up the debate."
—Larry Cohen, board chair of Our Revolution, past president of Communications Workers of America

"In this fascinating and insightful dialogue, the distinguished historian John Womack and a set of veteran labor activists probe the most fundamental of questions: How do we organize the twenty-first-century working class and give it the power to transform world capitalism? Are workers with vital skills and strategic leverage the key to a labor resurgence, or should organizers wager upon a mobilization of working people whose relationship to the economy's commanding heights is more diffuse? Or can we arrive at some dialectical symbiosis? Whatever the answer, this is the kind of constructively radical conversation essential to the rebirth of working-class power in our time."
—Nelson Lichtenstein, historian and author of *Capitalism Contested: The New Deal and Its Legacies*

Labor Power and Strategy

John Womack Jr.

Edited by Peter Olney and Glenn Perušek

A dialogue with responses from
Gene Bruskin
Carey Dall
Dan DiMaggio
Katy Fox-Hodess
Bill Fletcher Jr.
Jane McAlevey
Jack Metzgar
Joel Ochoa
Melissa Shetler
Rand Wilson

ISBN: 978-1-62963-974-1 (paperback)
ISBN: 978-1-62963-989-5 (ebook)
Library of Congress Control Number: 2022931963

Cover by John Yates / www.stealworks.com
Interior design by briandesign

10 9 8 7 6 5 4 3 2 1

PM Press
PO Box 23912
Oakland, CA 94623
www.pmpress.org

Printed in the USA.

CONTENTS

Introduction

Peter Olney

In August 2001 I left my organizing director post at the International Longshore and Warehouse Union (ILWU) to become associate director of the Institute for Labor and Employment (ILE), a California state-funded research and training institute headquartered at both Berkeley and UCLA. It seemed incumbent on me to try my hand at theorizing about the future of the labor movement based on nearly thirty years of experience in the trenches. So in early 2002 I wrote an article, "The Arithmetic of Decline and Some Proposals for Renewal."[1] I made recommendations about necessary strategic focuses for any renewal of the labor movement, which was badly reeling (declining density then hovered at around 17 percent of the total workforce). I advanced several recommendations, but one of the sharpest was for the need to focus on organizing in manufacturing and logistics, which I characterized as "Strategic Industries." In retrospect that was hardly a modest proposal, and it was also a proposal that underestimated the recent upsurge in workers' activity in the social reproduction sectors of teaching and health care.[2]

In August 2004 I ended my "sabbatical" at the ILE and returned as organizing director of the ILWU. I carried with me a "dowry" of research on the maritime logistics chain, hoping that I could motivate and inspire the union to once again "march inland" as it had done in the 1930s and 1940s, consolidating its strategic flanks by organizing warehousing and some manufacturing; all related to the flow of goods in and out of the ports.[3]

While there was interest in some quarters and some excellent organizing was done in bringing five hundred Rite Aid workers into the union at the company's Southwest Distribution Center, the union never took up the supply chain challenge—or the challenge of strategic organizing on its flanks.

Then I received an email from John Womack. I recognized the name—this was the author of a definitive work on the 1910 Mexican Revolution.[4] He had read my humble article in *NLF*, and Elaine Bernard, then heading the Harvard Trade Union Program, suggested that he reach out to me. I was flattered that he was interested in my thoughts on labor strategy. But then I discovered hidden treasure. Womack had spent decades researching and carefully considering problems of strategic sectors and strategic workers. He shared with me a very long academic paper that he had presented at a scholarly conference: "Working Power over Production: Labor History, Industrial Work, Economics, Sociology, and Strategic Position."[5]

This important work, impressive in both its theoretical scope and deep empirical detail, drew from outlooks as varied as those of John Dunlop (a well-known Cold War liberal) and such labor stalwarts as the Third International (formed in the wake of the 1917 Russian Revolution). I hoped John would soon turn this immensely stimulating work into a book. In fact, the Fondo Cultural in Mexico City had published in Spanish the substance of his argument in 2007 as *Posición estratégica y fuerza obrera*.[6]

In November 2009 the Mexico City government

awarded John Womack the Medalla 1808, a prestigious honor celebrating the bicentennial of Mexican Independence and the centennial of the Revolution. Womack won my deepest respect when he passed the award on to the embattled Sindicato Mexicano de Electricistas (Mexican Electricians' Union) who had been locked out of their jobs in Luz y Fuerza, the electric power system in Mexico City and many surrounding states. Professor Womack was not a sideline intellectual; he talked the talk and walked the walk, and that act cemented my respect and affection for him.

In retirement from the ILWU, in 2013 I circled back to John and continued to engage with him on strategic organizing and strategic position. I remained fascinated by the enormous power of workers in key positions in the economy. I had seen it up close in my organizing duties with the ILWU. I had seen one picket line bring a marine terminal to a halt and threaten the delivery of million dollars' worth of merchandise. I had experienced union-busting attorneys pleading with me to "give my client something" because the ILWU's exercise of port power had them over a labor relations barrel.

John and I exchanged emails, but finally I decided that we needed to record his outlook on strategic position and strategic workers. With my friend and collaborator Glenn Perušek, I wrote up questions, and in February and March 2018 I huddled with Womack, braving the New England cold at The Foundry, a restaurant in Davis Square in Somerville, Massachusetts. We tape-recorded two interviews. I prodded John to talk about the US working class and his view of the strategic worker questions in light of recent developments like the massive wave of teacher strikes. The interviews were transcribed and then edited by Glenn. Later we decided that asking some of the most thoughtful activists in the labor movement to respond to John's views would push the dialogue forward. We hope that what emerges in this volume is a rich reflection on how the working class can exercise its potentially mighty power, in industries as disparate as manufacturing, construction, or education. Few labor thinkers and organizers engage in the deep probing and analysis that Womack insists upon in his writing and in these interviews. The responses are equally engaging. Some of the best organic intellectuals of the working class—consistently seeking to raise theory to the level of practice—reflect on Womack's perspective and bring to bear their own rich experience in the trenches.

The publication of these strategic insights and methods could not be timelier as the labor Left grapples with the challenge of taking on the new behemoth of our economy, Amazon. This is an evil empire with a brilliant business model. John Womack has given us tools to ask the questions needed to unravel the logic of this company's business model and locate the vulnerabilities, the choke points, for strategic action by the working class. Amazon is a citadel of the online economy, but it is not impregnable; Womack and his responders have a lot to say about how to tame the Jeff Bezos beast.

We envisioned this volume as a back pocket reference and discussion tool for a new generation of labor organizers. Thousands of young people are seeking out ways to salt, staff, and organize unions.[7] They are attempting to grow and transform unions throughout the country—and throughout the world. This new generation, inspired by the two political campaigns of Bernie Sanders, recognizes the enormous latent power of organized workers. John Womack has been a good friend and steady ally to all of our direct organizing interventions within the working class; we trust that his strategic acuity and vision will be a force for years to come.

Situating Womack

Glenn Perušek

━━━━━━━━━

This modest volume records the beginnings of what might seem an unlikely dialogue. The form of this book is intentional. It sets out a dialogical, participatory approach to learning and thinking that is essential to the kind of democratic, active, mobilizing union movement we advocate. The voices in this volume do not always agree. The discussion reflects general agreement, which is then the basis for reasoned, respectful debate.

John Womack, the main speaker, is a rigorous, systematic and painstaking historian whose extensive studies of industries in Mexico advance a research program that draws on quite disparate strains of thinking from different disciplines and ideological orientations. But the result is straightforward: a focus on the unevenness of the operations of economic enterprises, on those moments in production or construction or distribution that present vulnerabilities. The question of workers' power begins with workers' relationship to the economic process itself. A supply chain is only as strong as its weakest link.

Professor Womack, the Robert Woods Bliss Professor of Latin American History and Economics emeritus, was

Port of Los Angeles, 2000: Crane operator moving containers. Member of the International Longshore and Warehouse Union. Photo and copyright: Robert Gumpert

born in Norman, Oklahoma, 1937, a son of the Dust Bowl. His people were farmers, and his early experience as a journalist immersed him in the everyday lives of workers and the challenges they faced.

Still, Womack has lived and worked most of his life at Harvard, the oldest elite university in America. After earning a bachelor's degree, summa cum laude, he won a Rhodes scholarship to study in England. He returned to Harvard to earn a PhD and was hired there as an assistant professor of Latin American history. His doctoral dissertation and celebrated book on the Mexican Revolution had propelled him into an interesting position within a hierarchical academy. A tenured chair at Harvard was at odds with his own modest upbringing and identification with workers, farmers, peasants. But it afforded him the financial security and time necessary to pursue his interests.

He was a rare young assistant professor who was promoted early and far, in part on the basis of his rightly renowned work on Zapata and the Mexican Revolution. He thus found himself financially secure and able to pursue his own interests at a young age. So, after the Zapata book, Womack dove deeper into the labor process in Mexico. Intending only a couple of years of study, he soon recognized that this subject was far more complicated than he'd at first thought. Two years turned into two decades—and more. The results of Womack's studies of Mexican industry form the basis for a whole renewed focus by the labor movement, and our scholars, upon the very production and distribution processes that are known best by workers themselves.

But that view is contested. Those in the executive suites of Fortune 500 corporations, many of whom see themselves as masters of the universe, believe their own leadership and the armies of midlevel managers that they deploy are those most knowledgeable and thus best suited to guide their firms.[1]

These corporate heads and their managerial subordinates spend millions of dollars in formal or internal education—the leading MBA programs across the globe are intended to educate these strata. Organized labor has nothing formal to compare. Yet we know from experience—and the historical record—that at pivotal moments in conflict, workers' knowledge of flows and choke points in production has been instrumental in the achievement of significant organizing breakthroughs. Auto workers' knowledge in 1936–1937 of General Motors' vulnerabilities is only a notorious instance of a more general potential feature of contention between labor and capital.[2] Organizers across today's labor movement can think of dozens of situations where they were able to use choke point power—or even merely appear to be ready to use it—to achieve strategic objectives.[3]

The employers certainly have resources available to study, mold, and shape the production processes of tomorrow. But, backed by a range of thinkers stretching from Aristotle to Dewey and Freire, Womack and his interlocutors are convinced that the practical knowledge of skilled workers themselves is ultimately the finest knowledge of labor processes.[4]

We have warrants for that claim. The interviews below were circulated in 2020 to union organizers, who held short reading groups on them. Listening in on these conversations, I was immediately impressed with the capacity of organizers (often with little formal education) to grasp both the conceptual framework and its variable applicability to work they've done. They generalized quickly from their own experience.[5]

Organizing in America

The respondents to Womack are seasoned labor organizers from across the movement (although several lead liminal lives between organized labor and higher education). Between them, the organizers have hundreds of years of experience; more importantly, they have reflected critically upon that experience and have played a role in the development of the labor Left in the United States.

These are unlikely interlocutors: The hermetic Harvard historian and a cross section of ground-level organizers and strategists from a battered but still standing American labor movement—what do they have in common? Plenty, it turns out. Both are interested fundamentally in power. This is a book about power—workers' power in the objective processes of production and distribution. Womack has taken up a monumental study, by drawing together threads of arguments and insights from disparate ideological and disciplinary sources (always a hallmark of intellectual integrity) and then systematically working through an understanding of choke points in a range of Mexican industries.

This was an area of some interest in the twentieth century, when the American labor movement was stronger. Womack had the good fortune to be able to study the work of John Dunlop, a Harvard institution himself (and briefly the US secretary of labor under President Ford in the 1970s); but he blended this with insights from labor organizers—and, always, from workers themselves.

But most of all, Womack the historian shares with the best organizers the single most important characteristic: narrative imagination, the capacity to put himself into the shoes of others. From myriad individual cases, he is able to generalize lessons and rules and hints—all of which organizers too discern daily in our work.[6]

So, to the labor organizers and activists who are the main audience for this volume, I say, John Womack is one of us. He has different craft skills but shares a mentality and value-based commitments with us. He may work in the midst of Ivy League capital and privilege, but this hasn't altered his lifelong commitment to rigorous historical investigations—always guided by both inherent curiosity and dedication to the improvement of the lives of ordinary workers.

Emergence of a Comprehensive Campaigns Model

The American labor movement suffered dramatic setbacks, particularly in the 1980s, that set the course for the subsequent generation. The period is marked off, conveniently if imperfectly, by PATCO. In 1981, incoming Republican president Ronald Reagan summarily fired the entire federal workforce of air traffic controllers who had engaged in an admittedly illegal walkout over legitimate grievances. This action hardly initiated the rounds of concession bargaining taking place against the backdrop of deindustrialization. Steel mill closures were already fully underway by then. What was less clear to us at the time was that we were experiencing not just a momentary adjustment to global competition but rather a restructuring of the whole post-1945 economic world. Since the 1980s, manufacturing once performed in the Northeast or industrial Midwest (or the Ruhr Valley or the Midlands[7]) had migrated to Mexico, Brazil, or Asia. With China embarking on a new economic path after Mao's death in 1976, a whole new field for the development of productive capacities opened up. To compete in the new, global environment, deregulation of significant industries abetted private corporate efforts to trim union labor's influence. The changed competitive situation left many US unions in a defensive posture that had been unfamiliar to them in the whole period of relatively stable expansion after 1945. Unions in industries that could not cope with technological or geographical change—or just the new, hardened bargaining posture of a wing of capital—were forced to merge with others as they declined in membership or went out of business.[8] Most of organized labor's efforts to organize new groups of workers—Walmart or the southern automobile manufacturing transplants or the burgeoning logistics sector—have not borne fruit.[9] In addition to the material changes—many workers, unionized or not, now faced downward pressure on real wages in addition to pension and health insurance burdens, the necessity of multiple-income families because of declining wages, and so on—a new ideological assault began. Talk radio became a mouthpiece for anti-state, anti-Democratic, right nationalism, a whole ideological seedbed for the movements that emerged in the 2010s. Labor and the Left have had no effective response.

To tell a long story starting in the middle: By the 1970s, workers' real wages (adjusted against inflation) had generally increased by 2.5 to 3 times, compared to the immediate postwar period. Since then, workers' real wages have for the most part stagnated. By the end of the decade, organized labor still represented nearly twenty-one million workers in the United States—roughly one-third of potential membership. Since then, union density has declined. By 2020, private-sector density in the United States hovered at about 6 percent. The overall figure is 12–13 percent, including the large swaths of public employees, including school teachers, organized since the 1960s. In other words, with important industrial, logistic, and geographic exceptions, the tide has gone out on unionism in the United States.[10]

Throughout the 1980s and 1990s, the American labor movement strove to develop new ways to defend its organizations and to reverse the decline in growth: from the corporate campaigning of Ray Rogers (P-9 in Austin, MN, 1984–1986) to SEIU's Justice for Janitors campaign; the defensive contract campaigns in Appalachia, the Midwest, or nationally; Pittston; the Illinois "war zone"; the 1997 UPS strike by the Teamsters; the Ravenswood contract campaign told so ably by Bronfenbrenner and Juravich, and more.[11] There were a handful of significant organizing successes, particularly by the Culinary Workers Union (today UNITE HERE Local 226) in Las Vegas. But the general trend was defensiveness in the face of decline.

★

In other words, taking on global capital is more complicated than it used to be. From the P-9 struggle in Austin, Minnesota, in the mid-1980s, which made Ray Rogers's idea of a corporate campaign widely known, through a range of bitter contract campaigns, often defeated (such as the newspaper struggles in Chicago and Detroit in the 1980s and 1990s and the "war zone" in Illinois), labor learned to fight smarter. We had to learn to fight smarter because the alternative was consignment to oblivion.

Simply as an indication of this new recognition, for the first time, the labor market was introduced to strategic researchers and the whole practice of researching corporate organizing targets more fully and systematically than had ever been done in the past.[12]

In this environment, the American labor movement has engaged in a long-term project of reimagining itself. I would contend that the labor Left, well represented by the contributors here, has come to a general agreement on an approach to the crisis. The labor Left sees building workers' power as starting with existing organizations—mobilizing union members in contract and organizing campaigns. This activism needs to blend into broader solidarities—with other unionists, other workers, and other popular interests. Organizing the unorganized must be a top priority. Building active, member-controlled and member-mobilizing unions, integrally connected with their communities, striving for good-paying jobs for all amounts to movement unionism (as opposed to business unionism, which sees members as passive recipients of benefits from elected or appointed leaders). Building strong, active unions also requires a comprehensive research and planning process. Corporations and their allies have simply become too sophisticated in "union avoidance" for labor to go on with inductive "hot shop" ground campaigns alone. But the solidarity built in any particular campaign needs to be generalized and extended. In terms of organizing models, the labor Left is pragmatic—sometimes running traditional NLRB (National Labor Relations Board)-supervised elections is indicated; other times market-based or even associational models are appropriate. Open, general workers' associations are actively under discussion. Finally, some conception of aspirational goals—politics in the broadest and most positive sense—must infuse labor. A revitalized labor movement needs to be part of an overall multiform movement for social justice.

The labor Left has evolved, since the 1980s, a comprehensive campaigns model as its general orientation. This entails a broader, some would say "modernized," conception of organizing. We speak of comprehensive campaigns that combine ground organizing, the direct approach of workers and organizers, with "air" elements—efforts to mobilize community support or hinder efforts of a corporation to use its business relationships to continue a hardened posture against workers attempting to organize.

Comprehensive campaigns mean strategic campaigns—and the study of strategy is far from a new one. Labor reads Sun Tzu, Herodotus, Thucydides, Caesar's Commentaries, and Liddell Hart's searching conclusions from his reading of military history.[13]

I myself conceive of the labor Left's comprehensive campaigns model as a research program along the lines of Imre Lakatos's conception. We share a set of normative and methodological assumptions, as well as observational hypotheses. These form the basis for whole areas of scholarly and practical research. Other approaches to labor contend as alternative research programs.[14]

Womack Adds the Dimension of Political Economy

Organizers and workers—inside unions and out—have for the most part focused our attention on the political-sociological aspect of organizing. We map out plans to build committees, develop invigorating activities to build morale, organize demonstrations or house visits—it is all about (interpersonal) activity. Womack calls for a regrounding. Not only are associational forms of power vital: basic, elemental power in the workplace is prior. Womack suggests that we not overlook this most basic kind of power that workers have: their daily work inside firms means that they have, in principle, a great and sophisticated understanding of labor processes. This knowledge itself could become another tool in the strategic campaigns box.

★

Aristotle made a passing reference to a myth that was already ancient by his time. What if a machine could be fashioned to move of its own accord? Hephaestus, the lame metalworking god, might fashion self-propelled tripods and even statues that could wake up and stroll across the room.[15]

Today, 2,500 years later, the world economy stands poised on the brink of a new arrangement between dead labor and living, between technology and human working power.[16] One hundred years from now, will the structure of industry and logistical distribution across the globe not have been fundamentally altered? Yet the irony of history is that workers who remain pivotal in evolving global logistics systems will have—potentially—more objective power than ever. The tripods might move of their own accord, but they'll break down and somebody will have to fix them. The unevenness of objective power, in Womack's terms, through time and space scarcely invalidates his insights. On the contrary, it confirms his essential starting point.

Jay, Maine, 1988: Members of the United Paperworkers International Union striking International Paper's Androscoggin plant. Photo and copyright: Robert Gumpert

The "Foundry Interviews"

John Womack Jr. with Peter Olney

OLNEY: How did you come to be interested in the issue of strategic workers?

WOMACK: In 1978, after ten years of the research that I could do while teaching, I started writing a history of Mexican industrial workers, 1880-1910. This wasn't to be a national history but a history of workers in the state of Veracruz, where several of the most technologically modern industries in Mexico then were transportation, textiles, electrical power, brewing, sugar, and oil, both production and refining. I wanted to go from the early stages of increasing capitalist momentum in Mexico, from the first major railroad in the 1870s, through British, US, and French imperialist conflict over predominance there (1880-1910), up through the Revolution. This was background to explain what workers did—and didn't do—during the Revolution (1910-20).

But I was trying to explain this history of Mexican workers mainly in a way that most historians of labor explained questions then, in terms of what they call social history. That is, ethnicity, language, social experience, social attitudes, and so on. I thought especially about internal migration, which I still think worked in Mexico rather as foreign immigration of labor works here. If people from Oaxaca, who spoke an Indian language, moved to work in a textile mill in Veracruz, where everybody is speaking Spanish, you might as well have been Italian and moved to Lawrence, Massachusetts, and worked in a textile mill there.

But then I thought, "Wait. What are these people doing most of their waking lives? They're working. That is to say, they're on the job, doing whatever it is they get paid to do, and so I wondered, what is it they do every day at work?" So I tried to write, what does a railroad worker do?

This was the problem. There is no generic railroad worker. They work in different departments, they do technically different kinds of things from department to department. I realized it's like work at Harvard. "I work at Harvard." Well, do you work in the Police Department or the Development Office ("fundraising," i.e., endowment accumulation) or maintenance or the administration or on the faculty, teaching? And *which* faculty? Law, business, arts and sciences, wherever—what do you do at work? I didn't know what to call this kind of question at the time. But I began to study what people who did know called the technical division of labor, typically organized according to different departments.

So I went back to John Dunlop, *Industrial Relations Systems*, a book I had read some years before and never quite understood.[1] I had ignorantly discounted it, but rereading it gave me light. Dunlop was an interesting guy, with intense experience during World War II in vitally urgent studies of industrial disputes in US defense plants. Then postwar, all through his long career, he had deep practical experiences in dealing with industrial disputes in all major sectors of the US economy, sometimes actually negotiating them, arbitrating them. There's a particular part in his book where he writes about different "contexts" of "industrial relations," i.e., the different kind of relations labor has in being labor in a society, for example, political relations (labor laws), or commercial relations (tight or slack markets), or cultural relations (the public's sympathy, or its antipathy or indifference).

Most interesting to me, then and now, was the context that he called "technical relations," that is, the actual technical relations that an industrial labor force has to maintain and practice in the process of work for the work to happen, for production to happen. I have to say I never liked the word "process" in regard to work; it's too abstract, way too general, incredibly far removed from work as workers know it. Already back then I tried to avoid the word, and just say and write "the technical relations at work." What do people do at work?

Industrially, even in a single plant, or station, or office, or dock, or data center, or server farm, or physically taking a set of things from one place to another, they don't do it in isolation. Artisans, dirt farmers, proprietary workers might work in isolation. But industrial workers work in cooperation, coordination, simultaneous or sequential or both, maybe in the same productive place or maybe in connection with another somewhere else, near or far. I want to say too that it's not a matter of "the point of production," an idea that I think came decades ago from Trotskyists—a mistake then, but now ignorantly, thoughtlessly used. At large in a nationally defined economy, in any industry, in any plant where there are technical divisions of labor there's not one point of production, but several, multiple points, connected, coordinated in place and time to make production, not a point, but as Dunlop called it a "web," or as we had better call it now for the sake of analysis, a network. So I've tried to understand this kind of relation.

OLNEY: Your interest was in workers' technical power in the work process.

WOMACK: Yes. I began to study Dunlop's concept of technical positions at work. He called them "strategic positions." They weren't labor's only strategic positions, these technical positions. He also described strategic political positions, commercial positions, social positions, cultural positions. But the positions that grabbed my attention were these technically strategic positions, which in a larger industry, a branch of material production, made commodities and surplus value.

I started to try to understand both technically and industrially strategic positions, first in writing about that railroad in Mexico, between Veracruz and Mexico City. And I thought I finally got it. To my mind the most strategic positions were dispatchers and shop mechanics, because without the dispatchers, communications, you'd crash the train, and without the mechanics, for repairs and maintenance, you couldn't take the locomotive or cars out on the road without the risk of a wreck.

This mattered industrially, nationally, because Mexico's most important business then was silver mining, on which its economy and its government depended enormously. Here's how: The exports of silver paid for economically critical imports, and the imports paid the customs duties that amounted to more than 60 percent of federal revenue. Already in the 1870s the silver for export came down from Mexico City on the new railroad for shipment out of Veracruz. And soon they had railroads north, to connect at the border with US railroad systems, to send industrial metal exports to US smelters. Railroads were then vital to capitalism in Mexico, so that if in a railroad company of, say, thirty thousand employees, you could organize five hundred dispatchers for a strike, then you could practically shut major operations down, which would in short order bring about a political crisis. That didn't happen, though there were big railroad strikes in Mexico in 1906 and 1908 that were deeply threatening to big business, strikes where the federal government had to intervene with barely veiled threats of armed repression. And as mining and manufacturing industries in Mexico turned to hydroelectric power, which happened there about the same time as it did in the US South, drawing textile mills from New England to the Carolinas, in Mexico too industrial capitalists connected their mines, mills, and factories to new hydroelectric plants. The big electric company, headquartered in Mexico City, had its power plant in the mountains northeastward, its transmissions running from there to several major mining districts and into Mexico City. And those electrical workers, who unionized—founding the Sindicato Mexicano de Electricistas (SME) in 1914—were able in 1916 to threaten the country's most important industry, mining, as well as light and power in Mexico City. And in the city they could do it in a very direct way, since there was no union railroad station, and to move much freight from one train station to another, companies had to use electric trolleys.

And so I thought, well, to understand Mexican labor organization and the labor movement, this question of strategic technical and industrial positions is critical. No matter what workers are mad about, unhappy about, indignant about, feel abused about, it doesn't matter until they can actually get real leverage over production, the leverage to make their struggle effective. You don't get this leverage just by feelings. You get it by holding the power to cut off the capitalists' revenue. And without that material power your struggle won't get you very far for long. So I then got more interested in the matter, not only for Mexico but in general as a question of labor organization, and that opened up for me a whole new area of study and reflection, because all along it'd been something very much on my mind, to try to understand the history of the US labor movement. And I began to reread some books and others new to me, and thanks to Dunlop, for the first time a lot of that history, back to Eugene Debs in the American Railway Union,[2] up into the 1980s, came clearly and powerfully to me in a way that it hadn't before.

OLNEY: There is a lot of confusion among organizers and activists about basic class questions. Maybe you can help clarify. In your view, what is a simple definition of "working class," and how many workers are there in the working class in the United States?

WOMACK: That's a good question, which I don't mean in the usual professorial sense, "I don't know." I mean it's good in that it opens up a lot of other questions, some of which I think we could know, but on account of US business and government nobody now knows or can know.

I would say the simple definition of working class, at least now in the United States and in most other rich, capitalist countries, gives you two working classes, roughly, simply speaking, a proletarian working class, that is, people working capitalists' means of production, and a proprietary working class, that is, people working their own means of production, which they actually own or rent. But this raises a bigger question, who is working, what does it mean to work? It's a terrific question. I had to take much longer than I thought I would to get far into it, and I find still there's no way to nail down a solid answer, even a very tight estimate. Thanks to the general probusiness legislation and budgets of the last thirty-five years or more, the Census Bureau and the Bureau of Labor Statistics have to deal with ever crummier budgets and can determine and count ever less.

I mean, I believe the statisticians are excellent and the counters are honest, but they don't have the budgets to figure out a lot of these questions. For instance, what's a job? As well as I could find it in the Census and Bureau of Labor Statistics, a job is, in my words, what anybody who receives income for doing it does. The official definition is explicit: a job is any work for which you receive a wage or profit. So first of all, rule out the work women do at home for their family; that's not officially a job. But keep figuring. You've got other people, say Jamie Dimon, or Lloyd Blankfein, or Trump, officially counted as having a job, though they're not in any working class in the sense you or I or most workers would mean.[3] But it gets more complicated. Consider another subject, not the same as who has a job, the subject of "the labor force." Who's in it? What counts officially, in the census and the labor statistics, for the labor force? It's the officially employed and unemployed, with no job but looking for a job.

But the official definition explicitly leaves out the so-called institutionalized population, not just students or people in mental hospitals but also people in jail, say two and a half million, or ex-felons, now at least fifteen million, by some estimates twenty million, practically banned from much of the labor market, and all the military on active duty (some 1,250,000). As best as I can put together various statistics, of a total US population now of maybe 330 million, you've got some 200 million people officially of "working age," officially counted from eighteen to sixty-four years old, though we both know kids under eighteen have paid jobs, miserably paid, or robbed, but anyway due wages, and lots of people in their seventies who are still working for a wage or a profit. And of all these 200 million, the proportion in the official labor force, employed or unemployed, has been declining for fifty years, so that it's now something between 60 and 65 percent. So I think you could figure a labor force in the United States now of something like 125 million. And in reality you could deduct from that number the people who are in fact for various reasons grossly underemployed, figuring that officially having a job, being employed, may mean working for pay or profit only an hour a week. So far as I can find, there are no official counts or estimates of them.

Beyond this deduction, you've got another, bigger deduction. That's a studiously estimated seven million who are just "missing," including, for example, ex-felons who can't get jobs, but also millions of low-educated males, white and black, who aren't looking for work, aren't "institutionalized," but have just quit. They may well have some real disability, at least, evidently, serious depression. They live miserably. They're not in the bottom 20 percent of income and living standards; that's where single women are, at the very bottom. But these guys, who do better than the women do, have anyway just bailed out. They spend most of their time, something over two thousand hours a year, watching TV or whatever they've got otherwise on a screen, about as many hours as a forty-hour week for a long working year would be. So you've got lots of people "of working age" that the Labor Department doesn't count. I would say that probably something like 110 million people employed in the United States are actually working.

But if you then look at the Census definitions and the IRS definition of employment, you get something even more complicated. You get employees of the kind we'd normally, classically, think of, namely old-fashioned wage earners. Then you also get "statutory employees" who are independent contractors but by statute are counted as employees. Then you get "statutory nonemployees," like real estate agents. Then you get "independent contractors," that is, doctors, lawyers, accountants, and so on, in other statistics counted more or less as "self-employed." And then you get "government workers," who are a whole other category. Altogether, whatever the legal distinctions between them, I'd say you've probably got something like one hundred million workers in the United States working for wages.

OLNEY: When you say "for wages or profit," John, what does "for profit" mean?

WOMACK: Well, at the top, financiers and big businessmen and businesswomen, numerically, relatively, very few, but below them are big-to-middling-to-small merchants, franchisees, and so on, or doctors, accountants, mostly small businesspeople in one line of business or another.

OLNEY: I've got it. Okay.

WOMACK: So you've got a round number, say one hundred million, but it's really divided. Thus, from organized labor's point of view, it's very complicated how many people under the labor law you can go after for unions and how many you might have to organize in other ways, not in unions, but in other kinds of commitment, leagues, congregations, alliances, to defend them as workers and earn their loyal support for unions.

OLNEY: A hundred years ago it was axiomatic on the labor Left that while we wanted to organize all workers, the strategic power of different groups of workers was different. The Left of the Second and Third Internationals didn't think about organizing merely in terms of the most oppressed.[4] It was also cognizant of the pivotal role certain workers played in the production process. Does this insight remain crucial today and why?

WOMACK: I think today it's still absolutely crucial, essential to the question of power, of labor's struggle for power. But I would make a distinction between the Second International, the Socialist International, and the Third, the Communist International. I think the more-or-less Marxist Second International's major emphasis was constantly on the political organization of the proletarian working class into socialist parties, to win power by elections, to gain political power, to make the national state a socialist state in solidarity with other socialist states. They were rather more cautious about union action, that is, labor's direct economic confrontation with capital. The great German Socialist Party wouldn't tolerate the new so-called syndicalists in its ranks, it expelled them for anarchism. They preferred laws, electoral victories, that kind of state security, Otto von Bismarck's "state socialism," or as the British or US later called it, "the welfare state." Lenin's definitely Marxist Third International, the Communist International, certainly as long as it lasted, from 1919 to 1943, was radically different in aim. Like the Second International, it was an organization of parties, not of states. But for its first twelve to fifteen years it certainly had a revolutionary drive. Its primary goal was Communist-directed socialist revolution in countries outside the new Soviet Union, fighting for international revolutionary socialism. Assuming deep, general capitalist crises and collapse, that meant the organization of Communist parties that in the capitalist collapse could direct class struggle toward the overthrow of capitalism, not to reform it into a welfare state but to overthrow it and establish some kind of ruling front or coalition for a working people's government struggling toward socialism.

But in neither case, neither for the Second nor for the Third International, was the focus ever simply on "the most oppressed." The most oppressed, they might well all have agreed, at least in private, were landless peasants. Marxist socialism didn't focus on the most oppressed, because however unjust their suffering, however deserving of justice they were, they could never electorally overcome or forcefully overthrow capitalism. The focus was on those most capable of gaining power over capitalism for the good of all workers, especially for the good of the unpaid, the workers robbed of all but a hope and a prayer of living to work unpaid another day.

The Third International was at least from its foundation to the early 1930s all about international revolutionary politics, for organizing parties of the working class able and willing to lead a revolutionary struggle for socialism. And most strategically these would be workers in production, above all in manufacturing, transport, and communications. In Russia in 1917 the Bolsheviks didn't spend effort on organizing shoe-shiners or barbers or bakers or street peddlers or rag pickers. They tried to organize and lead the workers in the great metallurgical plants, especially the arms factories and shipyards in St. Petersburg, textile mills in Moscow, and, in alliance with some socialist-syndicalist rivals, the railroad shops in all the major rail junctions. For the most part they succeeded, which was how they not only took power but then held onto the power against the UK-US-French-backed counterrevolution. These were all industrially strategic places.

So far as I can tell neither Lenin nor anyone else among the Bolsheviks ever published any explicit strategic analysis of work in production, for workers' self-defense or for revolution. But they certainly practiced it. In practice they knew well what they were doing. For example, I'd emphasize how Stalin himself first gained organizing experience among his in-laws in the Tiflis railroad shops. He helped organize various strikes there, so that he knew firsthand about transportation and its special strategic questions. After that, he went organizing in the oil fields around Baku, and in that very different industry he learned the technically and industrially strategic network. He knew intimately these kinds of strategic matters. Lenin was a very different kind of guy, a lawyer and a brilliant socialist politician. But the Bolsheviks generally, as they learned material strategics and taught and directed economically strategic organization, certainly acted in terms of strategic analysis of production.

OLNEY: This knowledge has been of great use in particular organizing campaigns. A famous instance is the US auto sit-down strikes in 1936, 1937. GM had only two sets of dies to stamp body parts, one at Fisher Body Number One in Flint for Buicks, Pontiacs, and Oldsmobiles, and the other at Fisher Body in Cleveland for Chevrolets. "It seemed logical then for us to concentrate our major efforts on organizing these two Fisher Body plants, since if we could strike them effectively, we could paralyze all GM operations," wrote Wyndham Mortimer in *Organize: My Life As a Union Man*.[5] Do these strategic choke points still exist? If so, where, and how can we organize the workers in those sectors and nodes?

WOMACK: Yes, I think those points certainly do exist. That strategic analysis from practice like Mortimer's on Flint and Cleveland goes back to the earliest days of modern industrial labor organizing. Debs certainly understood it on the railroads. So did William Z. Foster when he organized the great Chicago steel strike in 1919 while he was still a syndicalist.[6] From his practical syndicalist education, in the United States and Europe, he had thought it out, planned it, and he amalgamated American Federation of Labor (AFL) unions and previously unorganized workers all in industrially strategic terms to make probably the most revolutionary strike in US history. It failed, but it was terrific then, and it had great consequences later for the United Steelworkers.

So not only from the Bolshevik example in Russia, but also from the syndicalists then, like Foster, coming into the new Communist Party (CP), this practical syndicalist analysis and action became central to the party's labor-organizing program. There were others doing it too then, in the CP, or no longer in it, like Farrell Dobbs and the Dunne brothers in the Teamsters.[7] All sharp organizers were doing it or trying to do it. In their separate, ad hoc ways, AFL unions had also learned it in practice, especially the AFL's only industrial union, the United Mine Workers. But I think it was really programmatic for CP (or ex-CP) organizers, how they pushed it, taught it, most effectively in the new CIO industrial unions in the 1930s.

Mortimer's description is wonderful. There were similar strategic operations elsewhere in that period. Nobody had a blueprint for them. Organizers had to find for themselves in study and struggle where the right places were, when the best time would be. But they did it, by practical research and analysis. So they won great industrial power, less I would argue because of any labor law or politician than because of their power over production, over revenue, capital accumulation.

I want to insist, even if it's elementary and obvious, that it's most important that these technical and industrial positions, these choke points, are different in various industries. You don't have tool and die sets in a textile mill or a hydroelectric plant or a server farm, and in almost every industry, as I understand it, there's no single, complete technology at work. To make the product, whether it's a material thing, visible, tangible, say a car or a computer or a bridge or a skyscraper, or a material condition, invisible, even intangible, say communication, it's not just one entire, homogeneous, integral technology at work. It's always several technologies composed, put together. And wherever you put things together, there's a seam or a zipper or a hub or a joint or a node or a link, the more technologies together, the more links, the places where it's not integral. It is parts put together, and where the parts go together, like at a dock, at a warehouse, between the trucks and the inside, between transformers and servers and coolers, there can be a bottleneck, a choke point.

Wherever things connect, that's where they're materially weakest, maybe politically, legally, commercially, culturally strong, protected, defended, but technically weakest. Follow the admirable Peter Roth's principle: "If you build it, it can fail." And materially it will fail in certain places, or along them. It's hard to tear fabric woven whole, like Christ's cloak, all of one piece; it's much easier to tear it where there's a seam. You can pull a sleeve off your shirt much more easily than you can pull the back in two. But in any complex system, or complicated network, it may not be easy to see where the technically crucial links are.

Dunlop said that there's no simple manual for it; you have to do the research. I ignorantly asked him, in general, "Where are these strategic points?" He said, "Well, really it depends on the industry or the plant you're talking about." And he said, "It takes a lot of grubbing to find them"—his word, "grubbing." That means you have to have somebody devoted to analyzing the system's connections, finding the best link to break, which may well mean not just the weakest link, but the crucial links so weakly protected, so weak in the political, legal, commercial, or cultural defense of them, that in your struggle you can effectively for your purposes get to them, break them; or you need somebody who's actually worked at them and has the good class consciousness to think, "Wait. How does all this go together, how does it all work? Where can I really shut it down cold, cut off the plutocrat's revenue?" Those are the choke points, the crucial junctions, the critical nodes. In any modern productive system there are always some nodes, "vertices" I think they call them in graph analysis, that carry lots of "edges," even many thick "edges," heavy lines coming into them, and other nodes at the other extreme, with maybe only one little thin line coming in and another going out. What you want most is that node where the heavy lines, many heavy lines go, lines you can get to, where you can undo the system, a small network in a small system, maybe a big heavy system to undo the whole capitalist shebang.

I got the question from a good guy I know who asked me about telecommunications: "Where are the industry's technically strategic positions?" I don't know now. It takes analysis I haven't done. But the question is good, in that it raises another big strategic question, which is: What is your struggle for, how much is it for, how much do you want to shut down, for how long, how much damage to the system do you want to do? It's one thing if you've got enough working people for you and you're trying to seize national power, to gain enough control of the armed forces and the national police to make a revolutionary socialist government. It's another thing if all you want is to win a collective contract or enforcement of a contract or a raise. So you have to measure the damage that you can do with the backing you have and the benefits that you can gain.

OLNEY: Let me test out my own understanding of this and offer an insight from the Amazon distribution network. I read an insightful research report on Amazon. Because their whole business model is about timely and economical delivery of product, they are seeking ways to reduce their shipping and delivery costs. So they have set up a distribution system that has what they call "sortation centers" in every major metropolitan area within ten miles of Boston, New York, Cleveland, and so on. Rather than always using UPS or FedEx, these sortation centers sort product and then inject it into the US Postal Service or use their own delivery vehicles in an attempt to reduce the cost of timely delivery. The speculation is that sortation centers are choke points. If you could organize workers in these nodes and stop work there, you could inflict high economic cost on Amazon. Interestingly enough, these sortation centers might be more important than the distribution facilities that supply the sortation centers (The distribution centers also ship directly to customers using FedEx and UPS). The thesis is that the sortation center is the strategic node that you described.

WOMACK: That's interesting. Yes, exactly, a sortation center could be a choke point, a technically strategic node. But the decision between whether you want to go for a regional or a local sortation center, I can't see how it would be obvious, or even easy to figure. You'd have to distinguish the differences in technically strategic advantages you'd have between Amazon's regional and its local defenses and its exposures in a regional center compared with a local center, its relative vulnerabilities, the relative dangers to its business, how much, how deep, how fast, lasting how long. I'd guess the heaviest lines would go into the regional centers and out of them, but the number of lines might well be many more in local places, and the effect on customers much quicker and sharper. Historically in US labor it reminds me of the old brewery workers' unions, all local, tight, and some of them pretty radical, the key to them being the teamsters on the daily delivery wagons. Here, about Amazon, both kinds of centers are choke points. The main question I would think is: What is your struggle for, what do you want from the action, where and how much damage do you want to do, and how long do you figure you can keep it going? My irresponsible guess is, you want to find, if possible, two or three of the very busiest, richest local sortation centers, where Amazon gets lots of revenue from many impatient customers, and fight for these centers. I don't know what they've got robots doing in these places. The robot could run packages down the ramp right into the truck, but you can't load a truck, I don't think, by robot.

OLNEY: Not yet.

WOMACK: Not yet. Sure, if you've got everything of the same size, like the huge containers in Pacific shipping, you could just load the freight on pallets in the same dimensions and stack it into the truck. (One summer long ago I worked like a robot loading lumber on freight cars, same boards, same stacks.) But I can't see how that would work if you couldn't put everything in the same-size box, which for local delivery I'd imagine couldn't be.

You'd have to do the analysis. Robots can only follow their programs; and though they don't sleep, they do need maintenance. You'd have to analyze how to go around them. And I suspect the main problem here, in choking the distribution, would still be less a matter of robots than something pretty old-fashioned. I remember when I was writing fifteen to twenty years ago, trying to understand FedEx's main center, its hub, its biggest node, Memphis, how FedEx moved its shipments on land, arrivals and deliveries, trucks in, trucks out. You could see that besides the planes flying FedEx packages into the airport and out, they had to defend the trucks bringing freight to their warehouses and from there out to other centers or customers, and they were continually, really often, changing the highways, the routes.

The Teamsters were usually in hot pursuit, trying to find the new warehouses, the new routes, somehow to get to the docks and to the drivers. But the company, fighting hard, stayed continually ahead of them. So there was a continual legal and actual traffic contest going on, where the trucks would go and what kind of law FedEx could use to stop the pursuit. Now, as for Amazon, deciding between these different scales of operation, regional or local, if you could use action on a local scale to show credibly what you could do at other centers, maybe several at one time, it might well seem to make more sense to go after one of them, an especially busy local center, as an obvious threat to do more. You'd have to analyze it. Where's the revenue? What is your struggle for? What do you want and how much damage could you do to the business to get it? How credible is the threat of more damage? How much, for what you want, do you figure you need to do?

OLNEY: One major problem is dealing with the dangerous tendency to romanticize key sectors of workers, for instance, the attitude of "Occupy" toward West Coast dockworkers. But another danger is to forget strategic positions of different groups of workers. The fact remains that certain groups of workers have instrumental power in production or distribution processes.

WOMACK: I certainly agree.

OLNEY: And then what do you think of the distinction that Erik Olin Wright makes between structural and associational power?[8] Is that a useful way to look at an analysis of strategic workers?

WOMACK: Wright is an interesting sociologist. To the point you raise here, he had a particularly interesting connection in the mid-1970s, early 1980s, with a remarkable, brilliant analyst of industrially and technically strategic position— one of the very best ever—a young Italian sociologist into "systems theory," Luca Perrone.[9] Perrone, who'd evidently never heard of Dunlop, called it simply "position," assuming the position was in production, a position from which labor could disrupt production, and Wright himself, before he got into the concepts of structural and associational, wrote about "positional power," which he got from Perrone; it's the concept I see later embedded in Wright's "structural power."

Perrone was a very young man then and died very young in a diving accident in 1980. Anyway, as he'd sharpened his concept, he called it, in Italian, *potere vulnerante*, the power to wound, your power in production to damage the business, make the capitalist hurt. I'd contrast the point of this concept and Wright's point about "structural power." As an academic sociologist, Wright did interesting, influential studies of social stratification and related questions, but I can't see that in "structural power" he ever considered himself a strategic analyst. As for "associational power," it seems to me by definition not an industrial or technical power. It may well result from industrially or technically strategic power. This special material power in action, the force of leverage over production moving great weight against profit, just showing you have control of the best fulcrum, can lead workers in hope and courage to associate and go forward, appealing to popular morality or indignation for mass support. And associations as such can certainly have legally or commercially or culturally strategic power. But associational power is a result of strategic power. It's a consequence of strategic power, a derivative power. Even so, at least Wright promoted Perrone's particular argument on "disruptive positions" and got it into US sociology—though it seems to have disappeared in the cultural, identitarian waves of the last thirty-five to forty years.

Perrone is well worth reading, recovering whatever you can find of him in English in US sociology journals, or better yet in Italian. He is clear on this question of technically strategic power to inflict damage on revenue and bring the capitalists in effect to plead for relief. Whereas Wright, as an academic sociologist, was more interested in studying society as it is, explaining its benefits and faults and whether as a matter of social order and progress they make sense and are justifiable by some general standard. I think this is one of the intellectual hazards of being a sociologist. Perrone, on the other hand, though no militant leftist, was more interested in how systems break, how to break them.

Again, about "associational power," however derivative it is, I certainly admit it would of course matter in a crisis. You can't just announce, "The dispatchers are going to shut down the trains, the controllers will shut down air traffic, we'll hack the computers to shut trains and planes down," if it comes as a total surprise and everybody else in the country is against it. With civilian and military replacements the rulers would in a week find new dispatchers, controllers, de-hackers, and before long things would get back to the normal bourgeois contests. In a crisis you've got to have many people for your struggle, your cause, morally, politically, and that's association, people encouraged, heartened, emboldened by material power in action for them, but moved, mobilized, by appeals in civil society to interest or justice or both. But without material power in action, real force, all you get is association in action, movements, which in their heyday may be inspiring, but continually, always fade. Only with material power—not with it only, but only with it, on its strength—can you force change and keep it.

OLNEY: Today we are facing ever-richer global interconnectedness of the economy. We talk about global supply chains. Workers at different places in those chains are differentially positioned. What kinds of analysis, what kinds of studies are necessary for the labor movement of tomorrow to come to terms with these supply chains?

WOMACK: Let us set aside labor's political, legal, and other kinds of struggles. These all take their own kinds of strategic analysis, planning, and action. If we focus here on campaigns of struggle along supply chains, I think there's basically only one kind of study for them, to find the industrially and technically strategic weaknesses in the chains. Between industrial and technical studies you could draw an important distinction. Industrial studies examine how industries, different lines of productive business, connect with each other for an economy to function, [including] which industries depend on which others, like old-fashioned "input-output analysis,"[10] the study of an economy's industrial structure (or now, given globalization, the whole world's industrial structure), including infrastructure. Technical studies, on the other hand, explore how technical operations connect with each other for a given industry to function. In any certain industry or line of business, technical studies examine which operations depend on which, which departments (say, power) are necessary for all others 24/7/52, and which go together simultaneously or in technical sequence, or both, and so on, like old-fashioned "departmental productivity analysis." Or you could think of the difference as between extensive and intensive studies, between the broad and the narrow, the expanded and the specific. The range of your study then would depend on the purpose of your struggle, whether at its broadest, most ambitious, it's for historic, systematic purposes (say, the overthrow of capitalism) or less broadly but still for major purposes (on an international or national scale, say, in an entire industry) or for minor results (in international or national terms relatively minor, maybe insignificant, though certainly not so to the workers directly involved) say at a particular company, a plant, an office.

But over the last half century of increasing globalization, if you do a study of any major industry, in most cases now you have to do an international study. The major supply chains now are international exchange. You have to study the international logistics of the transportation, storage, and the delivery of physical objects and information. Most of these exchanges, most of the international freight movement and supply chains, are typically not a simple matter of two countries trading with each other, say X and Y, but a matter of several countries. I mean, commodities, so-called in the financial media—soybeans, corn, coal, oil, etc.—lots do go from an origin to a destination, from X to Y, from Y to X. But for manufactures now, products for sale in big national markets, the international exchange is typically not binational, from X country to Y country; it's multinational. The freight is different pieces and parts of things, or bits of information, from various places, X, Y, A, B, C, P, Q, R countries, parts and bits that workers at the end in still another country put together for the final products shipped to stores or sent to customers, or the information sent for informed decisions, maybe in yet other countries.

International transport and communication are no longer only essential accessories to production, starting it in the delivery of raw stuff to the place for its transformation and finishing it in delivery of final products to customers. Instead, they are in the direct grind of production so that in manufacturing the supply chain is now not only the first link in the productive process or the last link, delivery, but also a series of intermediate and intermittent links in the chain, the steps between the fixed stations of transformation. Consequently, supply chains are neither external (and never really were) nor just the start and finish of production but are internal to production.

The logic is the same as for the technical study you'd do of a plant or department or office, to learn where its technically strategic links are, where and when the place is strategically most vulnerable. Where are the docks or doors for deliveries and shipping? Where is motive and light power, the switchboard? Where are the generators? Where are the server room, the air-conditioning, and humidification? And the moving parts: Where are their connections, simultaneous and sequential, who tends them, who maintains them all, and where is their tool room, the HELP room? What's the shift plan? What are the various schedules and productive routes inside and out? Again, just as in industrial studies, in technical studies you need to learn where the various starts of production are; where the intermediate steps are, the removal of which would block most other production in the place; where is the final step, shipment, or "send," where all the parts and bits are finally just right, all put together, where the value is finally all in the product, but you can hold it hostage. Look in the simplest old terms, in high-cotton residential construction or fancy hotels, the plasterers.

Whether the study is extensive or intensive, industrial or technical, I think you'd have to start with "systems analysis" or "network analysis." Years ago I read a puzzle about a German city, Königsberg, along two branches of a big river, so there were many bridges to cross to get to various parts of the city. The problem was, if you wanted to go from one place to another, or to more places, which was the quickest way, how many bridges did you have to cross, the least number of them. It's the same logic, at least a comparable logic it seems to me, you'd apply in studies of work. The strategic links now aren't bridges (though I guess some still would be), but industrial and technical hubs, nodes, and vertices. This goes both for the study of global supply chains, international shipping, say, or telecommunications, and for the study of local interdepartmental dependency, to see where between departments or functions the dependence is tight or slack, where it's sequential, where it's indirect, i.e., through a connection that departments use variously but all need for production.

Of course, the companies that run these international chains and transactions or local internal motions and transfers in production already know their networks. If a company detects workers gaining too much strategic power in its established network—too much control over strategic hubs, nodes, vertices, cutting its rates of exploitation—it'll pay engineers (if it can afford them) to design or adapt a new network to escape labor's constraints, to restore or increase how much surplus value they take. It's what they call "innovation." So workers need to learn as soon as they can what the company knew when it installed the innovation, where the new hubs, nodes, vertices, are. And they need to learn not just where they are but also which have many lines entering and exiting them, which have few, whether the lines entering them and exiting are heavy or light. For industrial and technical strategy, it's the busiest and heaviest hubs that matter most, the docks for example, for deliveries and shipments, or the servers. Since the capitalists and their governments well know which nodes are most important, typically these are literally and actually the most protected by law, force, security, and physical or cyber-IT. You know very well, much better than I could know, how much police and military there is at big ports, maritime and inland. And just try to get close to a cloud campus or a server farm or data center. Even so, they're not invulnerable.

(a) You can always undermine security (at its technically weak links), or organize it for your own cause; and (b) the busiest, heaviest hubs themselves depend technically on less important but still highly valuable links. And at least for local purposes, for the most mundane but also often the most heroic action, organize the subcontracted, the guards, the cafeteria workers, the food truckers, and the shuttle drivers.

In particular I think the increasing electronification of security only extends capital's exposure to workers' technical disruption. Check the new Congressional Research Service report "The Smart Grid."[11] Without going to that trouble, just catch from the media all the hacking that continually takes place on the greatest international networks, like Facebook or the US Department of Defense. Or Bitcoin, for example: everything is supposed to be absolutely secure, but then hackers get to Bitcoin too, and not just for fun. "If you build it, it can fail." There are no perfectly, eternally secure hubs in any of these chains or links in production. There can't be, can't ever be.

So in this kind of struggle, on supply chains, on industrial and technical exchanges, these sorts of connection, I want to argue hard that labor needs network analysis to see where its industrial and technical power is. It needs to know where the crucial industrial and technical connections are, the junctions, the intersections in space and time, to see how much workers in supply or transformation can interrupt, disrupt, where and when in their struggles they can stop the most capitalist expropriation of surplus value.

Again, as companies in reaction try to beat labor by changing the chains or the technologies of transformation, labor has to keep updating its own studies, its own strategic analysis for new action. Industrial and technical "innovation," real or fake, total or partial and superficial, is a major way capital conducts its struggle with labor, a major way class struggle happens. It can look different in transportation, as companies may try to change their routes. It can look different in communications, where they may change the code, but the point is the same. Whenever workers show they've figured out how to put a wrench in an industrial or technical system, which capital has earlier put in place precisely to jump clear of their power in the previous system, capital then can go for yet newer technology or technical trick to escape the workers' new power, to get new means or a new order of production to render workers' power over the existing means and order obsolete. So if workers want to fight capital for the value it takes from them, they can't stop the industrial and technical education they need for the new rounds of the fight.

But I want to emphasize here that when the company makes a change in its means or organization of production (inevitably both), it actually opens a window for workers to get into it, a window that stays open until the change is definitely in effect. In this turn to a new or different technology and organization of work, on a big scale or only in some details, the workers who can get into the change—the earlier the better—can imbed themselves in it, lock into the training for it, take part in working out its defects, flaws, faults, bugs, glitches, actually engage in development of the new routine, so that they soon know better than the company's engineers (often initially ignorant subcontractors) how the whole system functions, why it can function, and where and when and how long it'd best to shut the thing down, partly or altogether. Just consider in computerized operations the continual patches and updates and upgrades, how often they happen, supposedly "for efficiency" (whose?), and the chances they give tech workers for "research and analysis" of how things go together for the system's production—and so how to take them apart.

The real question, as always, is how much your work- ers want to interrupt and disrupt, how far, and how long. To figure that out depends on changing conditions and purposes. It's very complicated, and as I'm insisting, it's not once and for all, for capital will keep changing its tech- nology, and workers have to keep learning how to get their own grip on it. But unless you have the power of disruption, you can't realistically develop any strategic plan, extended or limited.

The working class's deep, urgent need for this constant study of capital's continual industrial and technical reengi- neering makes me think it needs in practice a real center or a complex of centers for these kinds of studies, for research, analysis, and instruction, say, labor's institute of industrial technology, centers in every Federal Reserve district. Parenthetically, let me add, labor might well also found community colleges, a labor college for the study of capitalist exploitation.

OLNEY: With workers who are in a very powerful position in a choke point in one of these supply chains, how do we overcome the tendency of self-satisfied sectionalism? How do we get them to understand that they have to be part of a broader movement that goes beyond their own craft and their own workplace? That's certainly a challenge for the International Longshore and Warehouse Union with its powerful present and historical position on the docks.

WOMACK: That's a fascinating question. The question of partial bargaining or sectional bargaining was a great issue among the old labor economists. In Dunlop's gener- ation, and in the generation after him too, for example, John Pencavel at Stanford, it certainly held some highly intelligent attention and resulted in some very interesting studies of how sectionalism or departmentalism affected differentials in wages and benefits.[12]

Let me rant a minute, in full agreement with you: Taking advantage of privileged positions against less-privileged workers is obviously short-sighted, self-satisfying self-interest, at best a small, privileged group's self-interest, the best that individual workers or specific sets of them can do trying to be capitalists themselves: "All for me and mine, to hell with the rest of you." It's a version of an old Chicago school logic about unionism's evils, that the most responsible leader would show he'd done best for his members, taken everything he could from the company for them, if the company went broke the day the last member retired (assuming the company didn't fund their retirement). And I think in fact you have to assume that industrial or technical privilege, which is inevitable in any modern production, at least allows that abusive tendency to sectional selfishness. Only—some joke!—nowadays these wannabe-capitalist privileged operators find some international bank owns their retirement and plunders it for itself. Judge not by capitalist markets, lest ye be judged by them.

So really, practically, what can unions do about the problem? First, I think you have to recognize you'll never solve it for good and ever, any more than you can stop other human sins for good and ever. Second, if you want to fight it, you have to fight it constantly, and not institutionally, programmatically, by rules or statutes or committees, but by constant vigilance and resistance and the mutual support among all the concerned workers to stand against it. You have to make contempt for it the moral standard of the company's workplaces, make it your workers' second nature. Third, this takes education. I suppose at the highest level it's explicit political education, ideological education. There in actual classes, like classes in job safety, you could try to instill in all your members a serious, pointed understanding of a reality incomparably more important than a contract. I mean the reality of the working class, of which they're all a part, an understanding that would give them all their bearings about class struggle, how you don't fight capital individually or in little, separate groups, disregarding each other, betraying each other for a better deal in the contract—better just for yourself, your little group, or even for your union alone—because you can't win if you don't fight it all for one and one for all, the entire working class united for certain, deliberate specifi-cally working-class purposes. To do this kind of education, drive it home like attention to safety, I can imagine how hard that would be.

But there's another kind of education, implicit, folded into work, a kind of practical moral education, not in sit-down-at-the-desk classes, which can turn routine, boring, perfectly ignorable, but in an oath sworn among fellow workers of mutual support, pledges of comradeship, and meeting regularly in workers' workplace councils, to hear complaints of sectionalism, to treat cases of it as grievances workers can rightfully, in fact as a duty, claim against their selfish fellow workers. This is to make mutual respect a feature on the workplace's culture, to keep a culture of comradeship, where sectionalist disregard of fellow workers is shameful. I don't think this is silly dream-ing. I think it's most serious business. Ask a Marine about comradeship. Or read Fire Capt. James Gormley's eulogy of his comrades lost on 9/11.[13]

And here I have to say, reflecting on my comments earlier about Wright's "associational power," I can see better now it could be a useful idea. Only I still think the term is too academic, vague, too broad, and indefinite. Logically just from the term you're including capital as well, which also has "associational power," i.e., corpo-rations. I want instead a different word, a word with a strong, definite history, clear force and direction, a hard, sharp point. For me the right word for this moral power is *comradeship*.

And fourth, finally, some education in the technical analysis we're discussing wouldn't hurt these sectionalists. For their own economic good they need to learn about technical interdependence at work, in production. If they don't learn these connections, they'll pay a high price for their ignorance. They won't understand the economic gains they themselves, positionally privileged workers, could have in a broader-gauged struggle, gains not at the expense of their less privileged fellow workers but gains especially for them in this broader commitment in the struggle, gains that would make the union tighter and stronger in its constant conflict with the company.

These technically strategic workers, crane operators, others like them, who are highly skilled and seriously experienced workers, need to know on whom they depend at work. If they don't know it, they need the education to learn it. Except for artisans who not only know all the mysteries of their craft from start to finish, but actually perform them, everybody at work depends on somebody else, in modern industries on numerous somebodies. Those cranes need maintenance; I can't imagine the operators do it, but they depend on it, so that maintenance is also technically strategic, not in the same way, not as positionally concentrated as direct operation, but essential for steady, safe operation. You can see some technical power wherever there are moving parts. It's one of the reasons why I think machinists' unions everywhere, a trade union, were so widespread in industry, and so powerful. It started already when machines were wood. The first machinists were carpenters, for water wheels and cranes and looms and wagons. In transport, on railroads, in trucking—you can't run them without machinists. And try to keep a computerized project on schedule or a computerized network in smooth flow without "tech help."

But it's not only the technically privileged who need to know on whom they depend at work, the less privileged need to know who depends on them. I doubt they now typically do, especially young workers. Both the technically most privileged and the technically least privileged need to know, if only for prudential reasons, the technical complex of mutual dependence. And in the union or without a union the worker's workplace council should be teaching it to them. Workers in all positions need this kind of engineering education. You can't count on ding-dong lectures or jingles or pamphlets, "I'm my brother's, I'm my sister's keeper." Sweet idea, but within hours at work you've got dirty jokes about it. But once you see the technical connections of one job with another, who can foul or ruin or stop whose work, who can in fact endanger whom, high and low, back and forth, like in a team sport, a firefighter company, the armed forces, I think you get real attention to how much mutual dependence means, technical interdependence, the practical value and real advantage of comradeship at work.

OLNEY: You've spoken critically about analysis of worker power and position that focuses on issues of race and gender and social history rather than looking at work itself. How does this focus on pivot points and strategic positions that you are arguing for help us to think about strategic organizing campaigns, at Walmart, for instance?

WOMACK: Walmart, as you know much better than I do, is a complicated company, and getting more compli-cated as it moves into finance. But I think it does bear important comparison with Amazon. Both are companies using workers to stow and move physical products, like at ports; the workers are working at inland ports. I know the companies are shifting to warehouse robots to find and lift and move things. But it still takes live workers to program the computers, reprogram them, maintain and upgrade them, check on them, and clean the messes they make of things. Work-wise (i.e., aside from who owns the freight) both Walmart and Amazon receive finished parts and products, sort them, stow them, reload them, and finally send them, in Walmart's case to their hypermarkets, department stores, grocery stores, for retail there. In Amazon's case, they are sending parts and products direct to whoever ordered them. I think it's obvious that the kind of network analysis you need for global supply chains would be the same kind of analysis you need here for internal, domestic supply chains. Most simply you need to know which Walmart warehouses really are key, which distribution centers are the company's most valuable and vulnerable. At the retail stores, I'd figure, you couldn't do much serious technically strategic disruption, maybe no more than shut a store down for a day, and that would take a miracle of moral solidarity. (It could happen; I believe in miracles.) Operations against distribution centers would be harder but immensely more effective than trying to go after any particular store or set of stores.

In a general sense these supply chains, not only global, but domestic too, as they multiply and extend become more complicated for any particular business. In the old days, when you had great vertically integrated companies, where they shifted all the so-called transaction costs to transfer costs inside the firm, so that auto companies made...

OLNEY: The Ford River Rouge plant for example?[14]

WOMACK: Exactly. As far as I know, they made practically everything there that went into the thing they sold. That vertical integration, that comprehensive order of production, start to finish, certainly hasn't disappeared, but it's much less prevalent than it was forty years ago. Through this new round of capitalist expansion, "globalization," going back to the 1970s, most big companies (little companies too) have been into subcontracting, "downsizing," "outsourcing," vertical disintegration. But that only increases the importance of logistics, the industrially and technically strategic transportation and communication necessary for all these transactions. And on this point workers should never forget what communication really is; it's transporting information.

Since communications are much more open now and easy and quick, which means physical transaction is much more common than forty years ago, the work of receiving, stowing, moving, and delivering things is not only at ports (maritime or inland), but also at "the cloud," that is, materially, server farms. So companies that depend on shipments for their production, physical or mental products, things or information or services, or even that new commodity the rich are buying, precious "experiences," have much more exposure, not only to financial and commercial jolts in the markets, but also to industrial and technical disruption in the networked connections with each other. This matters all the more if the companies need delivery of things or info "just in time," and are in a race with each other to deliver them "just in time" to their customers.

Just think for a minute about that precious "experience" the rich want. It entails much more exposure to disruption than buying luxurious things does. As far as I know neither Walmart nor Amazon can deliver to the rich in their penthouses a vacation in Florence or Tahiti or a Botswana safari or a Montana cattle drive. These precious consumers of precious "experience" have to go there to get there. And along the way just a few technically strategic glitches would make the experience stink like vinegar. But this would be no more than trivial sabotage: the cook's booger in the colonel's BLT, anarchist fun, but no substantial or serious contribution to working-class power.

So, back to reality, any product that moves now, anybody who moves, goes through many more connections in chains and networks than a generation ago. It all involves who physically (which means mentally too) gets what, when, and what they do with it. Is it just in time to work or think the thing into a final form and deliver it? How much storage does it take? What are the necessary physical conditions for storage and work, temperature, humidity, etc.? It seems to me strategic campaigns, much more than they do now, should concentrate on these questions of transportation, storage, physical composition, i.e., putting things together, assemblage, and communication. There's vast historical working-class and engineering wisdom of practical experience, in analysis and action, so much reason to see how historical examples from old industrial structures and technology might, by intelligent adaptation, apply to the new technologies, and not only e-tech, but biotech too. You probably can't see it immediately, but you can learn where for the time being the new system is weak, vulnerable, and you can technically, strategically, take it down. I think at Walmart, at Amazon, at Apple, or at Microsoft, to name only some big, notorious businesses, the corporate questions of vertical integration, vertical disintegration, internal disorganization, internal misorganization, outsourcing, external transactions, make it all the more important that workers do strategic industrial and technical analysis for strategic action in their own defense. I would add, going further, going on the offensive, on a broad front, a working-class front, the broader the better.

OLNEY: There's plenty of talk today about the precariat which can shade over into a discussion of a relatively jobless future. It is not unreasonable to think that new technologies will indeed dramatically transform the economy, workplaces, everything. But we have been through profound changes in technology in the past. What do you see as the dangers and opportunities for organizing in the coming generation, given a sober assessment of the impact of these transformations?

Taxicab drivers today know, in a way that those running big unions do not, that both new companies and new technologies will be threatening their livelihoods in the coming decade. What should we do about all that?

WOMACK: That's a huge question. I totally agree with the way you presented it. Certainly, the economy, workplaces, the technology, electronic or information technology or now biotech, genetic tech, where they're able to grow live though not animate stuff for conceivably good purposes, will change a lot of the things. It'll change the way we make them and get them and use them. But we'd do better to think about whether the main question before us is the technology or the uses we make of it. It seems obvious; the last 250 years have been one big technological change after another. But if you think twice about it, the really big changes through these last two and a half centuries are not that many, not that often. The biggest, I think, would be in power—steam, electricity, its transmission—and in chemicals, and now bioengineering. Today many live in this ad-goosed excitement over what we constantly hear is a new technology, computers. But it seems new only as we see its new uses: e-cars, i-gadgets, "the internet of things." These things aren't the technology but the technology put to use, at least, in capitalism, made into commodities people will pay money to have. In fact the technology goes back almost seventy-five years, to the first electronic digital machine in 1944. And already sixty years ago economists and sociologists and workers were commonly worrying about robots, this then actually new e-tech making a machine do work people had done before. I'm sure that whatever newfangled twist engineers can give to electronics for new sales, the marketers/advertisers will keep calling it "new technology." That's like somebody in 1850 believing the steam engine was new technology.

So electronics—it's not IT, because the "I," the information, is not the technology, only the freight, the cargo, the load, the package—has been a standard technology now for some time. They find more and more uses for it to sell, for revenue, as they get pressed by labor or by competition. And the increases in the same tech's uses, for good or ill, will continue until there's some new technological revolution whereby, anyway in capitalism, companies can vault into new rounds of sales. I think basically the same is true of biotech. That tech goes back forty years, into the 1970s. And as we can read daily, it has new uses it seems every week, at least claims of new uses (often a year or two later retracted). It too no doubt will continue to produce new uses, for good or ill (eugenics, anybody?), at least in capitalism, if only for profit.

I think in considering automation, robots, "Alexa"— jobs, yes, but no human need apply—you have to start on the recognition that so long as we are stuck in capitalism, capitalist proliferation of uses of every technology for gigantic companies' profit will continue, whether the uses are socially helpful, wasteful, or harmful. You can't reform it, sanitize it. The only way to stop it is to stop capitalism, overthrow it. It's on these grounds I think it's a gross mistake on labor's part to look only at the jobs that capitalist e-tech or biotech does away with. Why not consider what kinds of jobs these technologies still require, or new jobs they will require, directly, or in prep, maintenance, delivery, in-house, or outsourced? And why not think what you could do with the technologies in another kind of economy, a socialist economy?

But here and now, in this capitalist economy, I certainly don't mean new technology will simply transform all the old kinds of jobs into new kinds, and just as many of them. The incredibly childish bourgeois economic arguments that new technology would replace all the old jobs with new jobs, maybe even open more, no serious grownup can now take seriously. New tech, now not so new, at least in its sixties, so far hasn't done that, and there's no reason for anybody serious now to believe that in its seventies it will do it, replace all the old employment with new kinds of employment. Increasingly, new ways of working for a living aren't even employment, W-2 employment. Under US labor law it's work as a contractor or self-employment, 1099 or Schedule C work.

I want to emphasize too it's important not to confuse industrialism, standardized mass manufacturing of stuff to sell to middle-class consumers, with employment. I think in worrying about companies like Uber we way underestimate how much industrialism continues, how much W-2 employment there still is in it. But from all the evidence and on the soberest analysis it seems pretty clear this is not the kind of production where you find old kinds of jobs replaced by new kinds of jobs. Industrialism may open new kinds of W-2 employment, directly in its vertically integrated, concentrated corporations, and indirectly (increasingly) by outsourcing to external suppliers that do W-2 employment. But the very reason for outsourcing is to cut labor costs, so that increasingly these workers are 1099s or Schedule C, whether it's all the time they work or the time they have to work on top of their low-paid W-2 job to make ends meet. So more and more employment turns into transaction. McKinsey, the monster consulting company, reported not long ago that in the USA well over a quarter of working-age people were working full- or part-time 1099 or Schedule C. This is what brilliant Chicago economists a generation ago called "matching," as in marriage, individual labor contracts, auctions, dating services, or pimps, certain very particular demands matching certain very particular supplies—or not (good luck!). Only they didn't have algorithms for it, which we do have now. That's how Uber functions. An algorithm matches a rider and a driver.

But here's where the question of new kinds of jobs gets considerably more complicated than just going from a past of human jobs to a present and future of algorithms, robotic jobs, "Alexa." Transaction requires reliability, clear, secure communication, no static, verifiable wavelengths or it won't happen but once: after fraud or incompetence, no deal. So who keeps the algorithm? Who keeps its quality from degrading? Who keeps communication secure? Who keeps protection tight? You have to have integrity to keep the deal straight. There used to be dispatchers, inspectors, and examiners. Now we have algorithms, famous for Bitcoin, but increasing in many other deals, all the more for the pseudomystical electronics of "the cloud" and "big data," gazillions of packages to send. But the algorithm doesn't create itself. Somebody writes it. Somebody tracks its quality; somebody makes the modifications to preserve quality. Nor does the algorithm protect itself against trespass or theft. Somebody patrols its use, reports misuse to the lawyers.

So here we still have human jobs, in production, maintenance, security, and of course, as always for bourgeois property, in this case intellectual property, punishment for its violation. (Would lawyers ever write a law for algorithmic justice, robots for attorneys, "Alexa" to do justice?) Plus, there are the delicious opportunities for income from piratical operations, hacking. This is now a real business, so you can now go online and hire hackers or buy logins.

But obviously, except for the lawyers, these are new kinds of jobs. The kinds of skill you needed for old human jobs won't match at all the kinds of skill you need for these new jobs. It's a caricature, but true, many old jobs took only a high-school education (of the old kind, the kind my parents had), and on a union contract some paid the present equivalent of $100,000 a year. In contrast, a high-school education now is pitiful. It wouldn't get you near these new jobs; it wouldn't even get you through the training for them.

And the world's demography warns this trend will accelerate. In the United States, Europe, Japan, most important in China, the biggest population in the world, the average age is ever higher, the average native older. We can see US citizens and legal residents at a productive age will be ever fewer in the labor market, too old, too overweight, too sick to work. To keep US production going, it'll take immigrants, young foreign migrants, the workers always most subject to superexploitation. There will be a US working class ever more subject to algorithmic matching, subcontracting, wage theft, faked self-employment, continual gigs, labor trafficking, no-poaching blocks. Some e-improvement of working-class life!

But robots always break down. Sooner or later "Alexa" loses her mind. You can repair them, reset her mind. But it takes time, and in the interim you have to stop; you may be lost. So it seems to me that in the coming generation the most important kind of mind or training for people who want to organize is some kind of engineering. It takes that turn of mind, that kind of training, to see into systems of physical things, even if the things are invisible, electricity, bio-cells, to stop them when you decide to stop them, for your good purposes, big or small. These algorithmic systems aren't real clouds, like the weather. They work because they're humanly set up to work, and whoever sets it up has to have somebody who will keep it set or reset it.

It's the engineering analysis of these systems of electronic or genetic command, direction, sorting, matching, that I think can show where strategic positions are and how you get to them. There's always a way to get to them.

So, yes, the precariat is here, getting by (or not) from month to month, living from hand to mouth, suffering all this debt and insecurity. But we see too that it can organize. Some can get together to write their own algorithms or get unions to help them develop their own communications, to organize among themselves, to learn when their contractor is most vulnerable, to strike then. Contingent labor never could organize the way the AFL or the CIO organized. Look back at the Industrial Workers of the World and harvest gangs. Unless, like the Farmworkers when it got going, it has a foundation behind it or the Catholic Church, I can't see that the precariat in any line of work could organize now for any standard National Labor Relations Board–approved contract. Even if it is, say, a United Auto Workers–backed contract, it can't be like a UAW contract. It'll be some other kind of organizing, these gig workers learning to take command themselves of the labor market where they work. I think it'd be a foolish mistake, a stupid surrender, a gross dereliction of duty to the working class, to say it's hopeless.

OLNEY: What do you see as positive signs of life in the labor movement, domestically and worldwide? And maybe when you talk about this, John, you could talk a little bit about your take on the recent successful strike by West Virginia teachers.

WOMACK: There are two positive signs over the last several years. First, most obviously, around the elections in 2016. The primaries more than the general election showed the spreading disgust, especially among young people, with capitalism's effects. Some young people now even say they're disgusted with capitalism as such, though I think most still dream that they could reform it, capitalism would let them reform it, and make its bad effects less harmful or even make it have good effects. To me, that's an illusion, but at least there is this spreading lack of trust in capitalism's natural beneficence. Despite all the hype about the American dream, many young people are ready to look realistically for something else. Of course, they divide all over the map about what something else may be.

But there's the second positive effect. Many are interested in what they think is socialism. To many, that may mean only a wider distribution of capitalist profits. But I take it for a positive sign, because with people who are willing to think about socialism, you can begin to educate at least some of them in what socialism might mean beyond, say, $15 an hour, and educate them how to organize for working-class power and where that could lead, for the good of all.

Besides that, many of the Sanders "democratic socialist" organizations have adopted the slogan of "Our Revolution." Now some Sanders people are talking about "revolution." I doubt most of them understand what that would really entail, how much it would take, how much it could mean. Still, the use of the word politically opens up the chances for a new kind of education about how much, I mean how little, you could change capitalism legally, how capitalism would resist legally and otherwise, and what undoing it definitively for something better for us all would mean.

OLNEY: What about West Virginia?

WOMACK: You know well the old tradition there of direct, working-class rebellion. That's the culture the United

Mine Workers came from, militant workers fighting like hell, dynamite and all, and not quitting. It's one big reason why they've fought so long so hard against the decline of coal mining. (The decline is inevitable, not because of tree huggers, but because of the oil and natural gas business.) But that culture of resistance and rebellion also, as you know, bred children and grandchildren, steeped in organizing to fight for their causes. To me, the most remarkable thing about the West Virginia teachers was that they made a labor movement effective outside the labor law, independent of the labor law. The teachers didn't have any labor law that applied to them or protected them. So, in disregard of long-established political contempt there for them, they acted on their own and had a terrific impact. I think that kind of independent, publicly defiant working-class action is much more effective than turning your cause over to the lawyers.

Those teachers confirmed to me yet again that over the last forty-odd years prolabor liberals have gone wrong in constant appeals to indignation or pity for workers, appeals for feelings to help victims. What works with working people is courage in action, the brave display of power. Once they see somebody acting forcefully in justice, they're much more likely to follow. You see solidarity. I think the last, latest great people's movement in the United States was the black movement driving the civil rights movement in the 1950s and 1960s. It wasn't hand-wringing and conscience-poking that won what was won then. It was public defiance and fighting the enemy where it hurt him. And since then hand-wringing and conscience-poking alone, Facebook movements, all those texted and tweeted cries of shame, haven't gained much ground for good. Scratch the surface a little and you see, capital and its servants are shameless. Among working people, seeing a big, bullying enemy of theirs really overthrown, not just publicly disgraced, shut up, but really shut down, done for, is far more powerfully inspiring and moving than a call to action online. It was when the teachers mobilized and intimidated the legislature that they brought everybody else out for them.

Moreover, back to strategics, teachers have a special socially strategic position that certain other service workers have, nurses, for example, or health-care workers, janitors too in big, densely biznified districts. Those people are socially, in some cases (maintenance in giant office buildings) even technically necessary for daily operations. Those teachers, as they threatened to disrupt the social lives of every family with children in the state, quickly caught public attention. It was in public action that they made people recognize how miserable their salaries were, how vicious the threats to their benefits were.

So, I think their public display of independent power and their public proof of the merits of their cause are the main lessons for labor in general now.

OLNEY: I'm glad you made those points, John, because I think sometimes when we introduce this subject of strategic position and strategic workers, people immediately think that we're solely speaking about iron and steel, ports and logistics.

And I think you just made a very good point that while teaching and the schools are not the commanding heights of the economy, nevertheless, those workers acting in the kind of solidarity they acted in completely paralyzed the functioning of the state of West Virginia. And all parents, workers, and other sectors were also impacted and affected because, you know, their kids didn't have a place to go.

WOMACK: Yes, aside from that immediate shock to those households all across the state, there was, as many quickly recognized, the much bigger, systematic threat that if the action went on for long, the kids were not going to accumulate enough school days to go up to the next grade or graduate or complete state-required credits.

OLNEY: Right. So I think you made a very good point, that this issue of strategic position is not solely a question of the commanding heights of product manufacturing or logistics.

WOMACK: You bet. And you can see it too with janitors. But there it is a kind of logistics. You've organized in those campaigns, where without janitors and maintenance workers a big office building is very quickly an impossible place for office workers to do their jobs. In navies they have to clean the heads. In armies they have to dig latrines and periodically burn them. An office building with the dimensions of a cruiser, where the employees would number many more than on a cruiser, maybe as many as three regiments on land, would be practically unworkable in two or three days if the bathrooms weren't cleaned—much more quickly if the toilets didn't work.

And cafeterias: When the dining-hall workers at Harvard went on strike in 2016, the students couldn't eat where they usually ate, in the dorm dining halls. Most of them could afford the scores of commercial eateries around Harvard Square. But since their boarding bills, already paid, covered meals in the dining halls, it quickly went from a dispute between Harvard and UNITE HERE Local 26 to include as well the legal problem of Harvard's failure to meet its obligations to the purchasers of its services, many parents, that is, the threat of lawsuits, more money at risk.

But on much bigger campuses, like Silicon Valley's, these logistical workers matter as much as foragers and bakers and cooks mattered to premodern armies. In these places, luxuriously isolated camps, logistically like military bases, cafeteria workers, food-truck workers, are technically strategic, because without them whoever doesn't have a personal chef on site can't work through the day. "Oh, well, order out, or call in the drones." But after a couple of days, without the logistical staff, there's mounting disruption, and the whole operation starts to go to pieces. That's technically strategic. It's only local. It's not a commanding height. But if it's where you and hundreds of others work, it sure matters to you how exposed its productive routine is to Luca Perrone's "wounding power," disruptive power.

OLNEY: What about the Fight for $15 and the fast-food workers organizing? This is organizing in a nonstrategic sector of the economy, so what significance should we attach to the success or lack of success of this campaign?

WOMACK: If it were only for fast-food workers, the campaigns for a living wage or the Fight for $15 are a simple matter of common decency, decent bourgeois justice. Simple justice. It would certainly make a big difference for people now making $8 or $10. But I don't think it would make any difference to working-class power at large. On the other hand, if it spreads from Burger King to big company cafeterias or hotel-chain janitorial services or a metro or state health system, to concentrations of those kinds of wretchedly paid workers, or if it spreads to networks of big business's outsourced, subcontracted labor, then I think the entire working class gains momentum and gains real ground, gains power so that it can force changes for working-class purposes. I can't see it's worth the cost to workers to go after small businesses or franchisees, except to make them cut harassment, maintain safe working conditions, pay the wages they legally owe, let workers quit to take a job elsewhere.

But if the movement spread to big business, say health-care systems, to Kaiser or, here around Boston, Mass General Brigham, or the misery of Louisiana's LSU hospitals and clinics, and if it coordinated these struggles in a conscious, purposeful working-class struggle, then it would matter on a national scale.

OLNEY: Recently the UAW suffered a dramatic NLRB election defeat at the Nissan assembly plant in Canton, Mississippi. Do you have any thoughts on that result and the prospects for organizing this very strategic piece of what I think you would agree remains a strategic sector, auto production?

WOMACK: Some thoughts, I must say not very deep or well informed. I read only what I found at the time in the bourgeois press and the labor press, so I have no inside information. The best sense I've made of it is that despite the years the UAW spent thinking about organizing the plant, which as I remember Nissan put in Canton in 2003, it made serious mistakes in planning the campaign and then ran a lame campaign.

Two things, I think, they did seriously wrong in the planning. One was they tried to organize a plant where the difference between what people were going to get in the union and what they stood to lose in life if they lost, was huge. At least it seemed to be huge to the workers there. They were altogether as I remember about 3,500. For them, in their minds, realistically, either they were going to win something more or they stood to lose everything. In a town like Canton, if you lose a job at a plant like Nissan's, there's nothing else to do. It's not like taking the risk in Birmingham or Houston, where if you lose your job, it sucks, but you can expect sooner than later to get into another plant. These Nissan workers were already some of best-paid blue-collar workers in the state. On the NLRB vote they were maybe going to win some improvements and stability or were going to lose their car and their house and have to quit their hometown, move away God knows where into exile, total instability. From all I could read the UAW's mistake then was not fairly calculating the risk they were asking the workers to take, not comparing what it was offering them with what they might well lose. This means the economic calculations alone were not right for organizing a new union in that kind of place.

Second, organizing in a town like Canton, you have to organize the community, which you can't do just by unloading money there. Union organizers in the plant, yes, but you need community organizers in the community for years before, expecting to stay for years after, to bind the union and the community together. And as far as I could tell, the UAW didn't have anything like that. The union did episodic charity, had some preachers and other worthies publicly in its favor. But Nissan easily discredited all that. "Look how much money they're spending here," it would say. "They're trying to buy you out. And afterwards they'll stop." So I think the UAW made some mistakes typical, sad to say, of big unions, totally focused on contracts, not looking in full at the local conditions where they're trying to unionize.

Recently, I read an old but interesting discussion where Communications Workers of America (CWA) organizers argued that point very well. Their example was a case at a state university in East Texas, 1987, not very pertinent to Canton, 2017. But the point I think is practically the same as the point I want to make about Canton. The workers worked in the university's food services and belonged to a CWA state employees' union, and the administration was acting to replace them with subcontracted labor, of course not union. The workers held together, fought in unity, got terrific help from other unions and pro-union organizations around the country, saved their jobs, and won, for CWA Local 6186 in Nacogdoches. The main reason they could fight that way was, many of them already from fifteen years before had been deep in a local NAACP struggle for civil rights at the university. You had plenty of people then used to fighting for themselves, their fellow workers, their common good, well before you tried for a union. They were veterans in the struggle; they continually raised hell for their rights at the university long before the union, which I haven't heard about in Canton. So I think you could have bet before it started that the UAW campaign in Canton probably wasn't going to work, however excited pro-union liberals were about it.

Besides, it seems the Canton organizing committee wasn't much on the ABCs of organization. It didn't extend its operations across all the plant's departments, and even in the departments where it was trying to operate, its organizers were not uniformly strong in their commitments. You had some brave, good fighters. You also had some slackers.

OLNEY: I think you pointed to two of the factors. I heard from talking to people on the ground that this—and this is where your comparison of relative things to be gained versus things to be lost, that the company presently offers this benefit of leases of company vehicles for employees and their family members. Somebody explained to me that the loss of such a vehicle is basically the loss of work in that area because there's no public transportation.

WOMACK: Exactly. You'd have to walk to get your groceries.

OLNEY: So that was a huge benefit that was threatened, not explicitly by the company but implicitly.

WOMACK: Exactly.

OLNEY: And second, this point you made to close here is extremely important because I also talked to people on the ground and there was really nothing going on inside the plant in terms of fighting over the day-to-day issues that workers faced, which builds a sense of power and organization.

WOMACK: You know incomparably better than I what went on inside. But again you're absolutely right, I think, that organizers need daily de facto militant steward patrols and defiance of management's injustices to build the unity before the union.

OLNEY: None of that really happened inside the plant, as opposed to the successful Smithfield campaigning in Tar Heel, North Carolina. They won in 2008, but that was preceded by a long history of struggling around all kinds of issues inside and outside the plant. So I think you're making solid points in terms of the problems with organizing in that environment.

You have already spoken on the openness of young people in this country to the idea of socialism and discussion of socialism. Would you talk more on your observations about labor for Bernie or the prognosis for labor politics going forward?

WOMACK: One point I do want to make is that so long as the Democratic National Committee follows Wall Street's directions, respects its vetoes, the DNC will be pestilential to the labor movement and the working class at large. The more that unions for Bernie can do to separate themselves from the DNC and its puppets in state Democratic committees, the better I think they can do.

Local Democratic organizations need to be built that actually support labor, not just unions and their contracts, but working people of all kinds, in all their troubles. At the top of the list is debt—public debt, which probusiness politicians use to justify cutting public services; and workers' private debts, for necessities like housing and health. Such organizations can help the labor movement protect itself politically.

If unions for Bernie can clearly and truthfully explain that "the middle class" is not a US birthright or civil right to complain about losing, but a blindfold on "working people," a brainwash to make them think they can get it made, forever, get a secure lock on comfort in this capitalist madhouse, the better I think unions will do for themselves and for laborites in government. But again, I want to emphasize, I think the best way to get working people's solid support is by displaying effective power for them, at least use their power to fight for more than their contracts, to fight publicly for all the working people whose support they want and need. Until Democratic politicians see that constituents are not all dupes, that working people will follow the display of effective power for their concerns, they're not going to do more than they're doing now, which is mostly simple moderate Republicanism, or nothing, or worse. To some extent that's how the Tea Party did it for "free enterprise," for capitalism. It didn't compromise. It scared local politicians, state politicians, national politicians, made them go whole hog for business, against working people and unions. Look how much it's won for business, how many working people it's trashed!

Until organized labor can show effective power in struggle, not just for unions but for the working classes as a whole, it will continue to lose support. Labor needs to be able to win power by industrial or technical disruption or otherwise, acting under the labor law or independent of it. Until then, this society will go farther to the big, barking, biting dogs. Politically I hope it can struggle for new representation, either in the Democratic Party or another party. It would not have to win majorities to do good for working people.

Ever since the New Deal, the labor movement has worshipped at the altar of the National Labor Relations Act. For that idolatry, for the last forty years it's been facing the Political Wrath of God, in plagues of Rabid Republicanism and Mealy Democratism. Organized labor would do better if it got over the illusion that working-class power in the United States ever was or is now or in the future can be in office or in a contract or in court. Office, in itself, we've seen is not reliably effective. If your guys here and there win elections, win appointments, you have to keep really powerful pressure on them, or the lobbyists and lawyers and pollsters take over and tell them what they can and can't do to stay where they are. Fundamentally, organized labor's political power comes from working people. It is only that power that results in pro-union politics and pro-union officials. Like in West Virginia, the more power you can show, the more official power bends before your drive. Labor politics is hopeless if it's only for an accommodation with capitalism, in "the middle class." Just think of the submission to the rich and the irresponsibility toward the poor, the two-faced shame, in that kind of politics.

OLNEY: In the wake of West Virginia, teachers' activism spread to your home state of Oklahoma.

WOMACK: Far apart as they are, West Virginia and Oklahoma have some similar historical streaks. When Oklahoma was still Indian Territory, more than a century ago, and for decades into statehood, the United Mine Workers had a terrific, militant base there, District Twenty-One, in coal-rich

Pittsburg County, a major power all over the eastern third of
the state and into Arkansas. And as in West Virginia, some
miners' children got out of the mines, became teachers. My
eighth-grade Oklahoma history teacher came from that coal
country, wrote his PhD thesis at OU on coal and the union.
He taught us before we knew what we were learning a state
history of the Indian Trail of Tears, of black struggles for
rights, and of working-class struggles for justice. Maybe
because so many working people had children who become
teachers, the teachers' union in Oklahoma was for decades
the main power in organized labor. Republicans have done
their best to beat it to death, but it's still one of the state's
most serious labor organizations. In seventy-seven coun-
ties you must have at least five hundred school districts,
and many of them on their budgets can run only miserable
schools. Homebrew drugs plague them too, awful in the
rural districts, some where most working-age adults are
gone, dead, in jail, or given up, nobody but grandparents
and kids left. In the teachers' struggle, besides miserable
wages and benefits, they don't even have the kind of legal
protection they deserve, simple legal protection of their
jobs, for their work. Nevertheless, I think that as in West
Virginia, the Oklahoma teachers do have socially important
strategic power, and I'd rejoice if they turned it into something serious there.

OLNEY: I think it's exciting to see that, in the parlance of
modern-day electoral politics, two of the deepest red zones
in the country may become *real* red zones.

WOMACK: Yes. That would be glory.

OLNEY: So finally, you've written a great book that has
been published in Mexico called *Posición estratégica y
fuerza obrera* (Strategic position and working-class power).

When is this book going to be translated and published for English readers?

WOMACK: God knows. I can only hope, and I hope soon. First, I have to finish writing a book I'm at now, on very different questions in Mexican history. Then if I still have any mental clarity and eyes and both hands that work, I can go back to "Strategic Position," which is all there in English sitting in the computer. It wouldn't take long to revise a few pages and update the last part, on the last ten years. We'll see then if I can interest a US publisher in it.

OLNEY: We call this the "Foundry Interviews" in honor of the restaurant we're at here in Davis Square, Somerville, Massachusetts, and also the topic we're dealing with, and because it is so crucial and so fundamental to the future of the working-class movement in this country. So thank you again for spending time answering these questions. We hope to transcribe them and turn them into something that can be useful, particularly to young people who are doing working-class organizing.

Detroit, Michigan, 1982: A worker, and member of the United Auto Workers, on an auto assembly line. Photo and copyright: Robert Gumpert

Should Spartacus Have Organized the Roman Citizenry Rather Than the Slaves?

Bill Fletcher Jr.

Strategy begins with an assumption about representation. To borrow from Mao Zedong, we must first and foremost identify who are "the people" to whom everyone refers. Mao's contribution in this matter was to note that "the people," at least at the political level, is a term that does not have a permanent existence. It is also not demographic. It refers to the oppressed majority in any society who are *and act upon* their contradictions with the forces of oppression and domination. This means that the notion of the people changes over time depending to a great extent on the nature of the enemy or opponent at any one moment, and the stage of the struggle.

I start there because Womack's interview revolves around the question of what organized labor should be doing today and its relationship to the rest of the working class. Dr. Womack carefully identifies the segments of the working class, and particularly organized labor, that are best positioned to influence capital and to gain some level of collective power. It is these sectors, he stresses, that need greater organization and attention by organized labor.

The sectors that have the most influence due to their location in the production process, Dr. Womack argues, are in areas such as logistics and high technology. Drawing on a historical analysis that notes the importance, over time, of different segments of the economy, Womack points out that the concept of the "most oppressed" part of the working class has not been the criteria for organizing in order to build working-class power.

The notion of "most oppressed" is a complicated concept. The Left and, specifically the Left within labor, has always had to make certain strategic decisions about where it should concentrate its resources. But that decision cannot be based exclusively on an appraisal of which sectors will have the greatest ability to defeat or blunt the power of capital. Sometimes that decision needs to emerge from an analysis of which sectors of society are *in struggle*.

Though the Russian Revolution has been called a "workers' revolution," it was a revolution of workers and peasants led by a working-class revolutionary party. Had the Bolsheviks not been able to win significant segments of the peasantry, they would have been crushed. In the case of the Chinese Revolution this issue reemerged. The leadership, under Mao, unapologetically focused on the peasantry, who constituted the overwhelming majority of the country, though Mao emphasized the need for working-class leadership.

I would argue that in neither case did these parties look at the peasantry as a base of last resort; instead they were seen as an essential base that could bring about necessary change. Mao and others identified the so-called spontaneous uprisings that took place in the countryside in the mid-1920s, which, he argued, needed to be a focus of the work of the Communist Party.

In the United States there is an interesting example of the complication in identifying strategic targets. Dr. Womack correctly speaks to the targets of attention that the Congress of Industrial Organizations (CIO) chose in the 1930s. But let's shift to 1946 and Operation Dixie, the CIO's attempt to organize the South. There were many problems with this campaign, but here we'll focus on one. The CIO chose the textile industry, believing that as went textile, so went the rest of the South. But the choice of textile was problematic from the start due to racist oppression within that sector and paternalist management of the workforce. In fact, Left-led unions in the South had far more success with other sectors where workers were in motion and there were more diverse workforces, a fact for which they have been given limited credit.

In the nonrevolutionary situation of today's USA, the Left is contemplating how to build mass, working-class power. How, it asks, can organized labor renew itself and which sectors should it seek to organize to blunt the power of neoliberal capital?

Strategy, then, needs to begin with an assessment of the state of "the people" and seek to understand which sectors are in motion and which are not; which sectors may be in a better position to create a power ripple and which are not. Unless these questions are examined *jointly*, there is a significant danger that a "strategic sector" may turn out to be one that looks out for its own interests— defined in any number of ways—sometimes in the most toxic manner, for example, the demand of white mine workers in South Africa in the 1920s for "Workers of the World Unite and Fight for a White South Africa!"

Trade Union Consciousness vs. Class Consciousness

Womack makes a strong argument in favor of class consciousness over sectoral or trade union conscious-ness, emphasizing a *culture of comradeship* or what my friend and coauthor Dr. Fernando Gapasin calls a *culture of solidarity*.

Building this culture of comradeship or culture of solidarity, however, must begin not only with a recognition of the danger of falling prey to sectionalism, but a recognition that class struggle is not necessarily the same thing as workplace struggle. The labor Left at its best has recognized that the objective of trade unions and the labor movement as a whole must look out for the total worker (to borrow from the late Teamster leader Harold Gibbons from St. Louis) and the broader working class.[1] The struggles undertaken by workers may or may not be in the workplace, but class struggle exists irrespective of whether the specific struggles take place in community-based areas, the electoral arena, or some other site of struggle. The question revolves around how the interests of these contending classes are engaged and whose interests come to dominate.

Such struggles can be strategic in that they shift the larger societal balance of power. This is obviously the case in certain elections, but one can also examine struggles such as the South African antiapartheid struggle—particularly in the 1980s—where the mass battles in the townships to make South Africa ungovernable were directly linked with workplace struggles led by newly independent black trade unions.

Jobs and Joblessness

While I am not apocalyptic, I believe Womack is a bit more sanguine about the future of jobs than am I.

It is absolutely the case that capitalism has brought with it various technological changes that have aimed to increase productivity and weaken the power of workers. With these various technological changes entire workforces have lost out, while new sectors have emerged.

The current situation appears a bit more complicated. The introduction of new technologies, specifically automation and robotization, has neither brought about an immediate collapse in the workforce nor introduced readily accessible living-wage employment. Ironically, it appears that over the last several years, increased automation has not increased productivity for capital but is changing the nature of work. It is bringing with it an increase in low-skilled, low-paid employment on one end, and higher-skilled, higher-paid employment on the other end, though for fewer workers. It is not creating work for those displaced and, certainly at the high end, is not creating work for the undereducated.

Changing technology has also changed the manner in which work is done. This can mean a reduction in the workforce (e.g., automation of longshore work dramatically reducing work) or an alteration of work (e.g., the reorganization of the taxi industry with the growth of Uber and Lyft). This introduction of new technology is the result of class struggle and the bitter efforts of capital to weaken the working class and to reduce the numbers of workers it must compensate.

This situation creates a setting for mass redundancy and further pauperization. It makes the challenge facing more stable sections of the working-class even more urgent in addition to unstable or contingent segments. This creates major organizing challenges for the Left and organized labor. To what extent does the working class becoming more informalized interfere with the growth of class consciousness? To what extent does that create a tension whereby informalized segments see themselves at odds with those who hold formal employment? And to what extent do the workers in the formal and more stable economy look down their noses at those who they may have come to believe hold them back from regaining their so-called middle-class status?

Our approach to strategy and class struggle must look broader than the question of strategic segments of the working class. We must confront the question of *sites of struggle*. We must also recognize that one cannot expect capital to replace existing jobs with comparable jobs or higher-paying positions overall. As repeatedly pointed out, many of the higher-waged jobs that began disappearing in the 1970s and 1980s were not higher-waged jobs in the 1930s, and not simply because of the Depression. These jobs altered when they were unionized through intense struggle.

Yet there is another factor that we can only touch on but needs deeper examination. To borrow from the late Egyptian economist and global thinker Samir Amin, the welfare state was only possible based on cheap oil. His statement is quite profound. The low cost of extractive materials, largely due to colonialism, neocolonialism, and the superexploitation of workforces in the Global South, allowed capital in the Global North to make certain concessions to their respective domestic class struggles. As that situation has altered and as global capitalism has morphed, capital has—internationally—undertaken a war against workers, seeking to drive down their living standards. As a result, elements of the Global South—speaking metaphorically—can be found in the Global North; and elements of the Global North can be found in the Global South.

To the extent to which we do not emphasize class consciousness and internationalism, the working class can fall on its knees before various forms of right-wing populism that propose to return to an enlightened racist, sexist, and jingoistic age, believing that this will be the chance for a restoration of what was lost.

There is an additional point about jobs and joblessness that I hasten to add. The late Tony Mazzocchi, longtime trade unionist and founder of the Labor Party in the USA in 1996, repeatedly emphasized that jobs, as a category, do not exist in the abstract. Society has work to be done, and this necessitates jobs. This means that certain forms of work that are today not classified as "jobs" could easily be so classified. One example he offered was that of the GI Bill in the aftermath of World War II. This legislation provided significant benefits to many US veterans such that they could go to college or vocational school, buy homes, and more, elevating them out of poverty. That the GI Bill was implemented in a racially discriminatory fashion must be noted, but Mazzocchi's point was that recipients of the GI Bill were not treated as loafers; their time in school was legitimated by the larger society. It was "work."

Using that as a model, much of the work that is frequently imposed on families to perform, such as childcare and eldercare, could and should be treated as legitimate, dignified work that pays a living wage. This will only happen through struggle and not through expectations of divine or charitable intervention.

Race, Gender, and Class

In the "Foundry Interviews" there is a curious, if not interesting, question posed to Dr. Womack about matters of race, gender, and social history versus a focus on work (43). Womack answers the question at the level of a structural analysis about work but does not address matters of race and gender directly. Herein lies part of the problem.

Identifying sites of struggle and sources of motion must be at the core of one's overall strategic analysis. And sites of struggle, precisely because they need not be workplaces, can unfold in such a way that they involve various segments of the working class whereby the struggle is not necessarily seen—at least initially—as a working-class struggle but is objectively a manifestation of the class struggle. The sanitation workers in Memphis, Tennessee, in 1968 were not central to the production process, but their struggle was central to the energizing of a (partially) fused black freedom movement and workers' movement at that moment in that city. The black freedom movement was not an ancillary social movement but was central to the larger class struggle in the USA. In that sense, the failure of organized labor to embark on a major public-sector organizing effort in the South in the aftermath of the Memphis sanitation workers strike, an effort that would have tapped into the larger African American community in the South, was a terrible missed opportunity, the ramifications of which we continue to live with.

Race and gender are not identity questions. They speak to a specific set of contradictions and forms of oppression that are central to actually existing capitalism. An analysis aimed at the construction of a progressive, if not revolutionary strategy for labor must, as a result, see in the struggles that emerge among the racially, nationally and gender oppressed, sources of strength and renewal rather than struggles to either be ignored or to be treated as charity cases.

Womack correctly identifies the weaknesses in the United Auto Workers' efforts in organizing Nissan workers in Canton, Mississippi. While there were and are many problems inherent in organizing workers in transplanted facilities where the new employment is dramatically different from other available employment, Womack hits the nail on the head in identifying the need for a sustained engagement with the workers and their community. What I believe needs to be added is that such a sustained effort would necessitate the UAW thinking about a different paradigm of trade unionism, a social justice unionism, to be exact, that engages the workers, their families, and their communities in the broader class struggle. Central to that struggle in the South is one that takes on racist oppression. And in taking it on, that struggle or set of struggles help to make a mark on the nature of the union—and unionism—in that context and for that working-class population. That lesson was correctly learned in the victory by the United Food and Commercial Workers in organizing workers at the Smithfield facility in Tar Heel, North Carolina.

★

We don't know for sure what Spartacus was thinking. At one level a mobilization of the Roman citizenry might very well have brought Rome to its knees. But Spartacus was organizing the slaves who were an oppressed population constantly in action and revolt. While he and his uprising failed, he placed himself within *the people* who were in motion and, indeed, came close to defeating the Roman Republic. In fact, the outcome might have been quite different: ask the Haitians what happened in 1803.

Harlan, Kentucky, 1974: The United Mine Workers of America, having called a day of mourning for miners killed in the mines, brought thousands of members to Harlan in support of strikers at the Brookside Mine. Photo and copyright: Robert Gumpert

Relaying These Insights Is More Urgent Now Than Ever

Dan DiMaggio

As the US labor movement has largely abandoned the strike weapon, and the organized working class has continued to shrink, it's become ever harder for newer generations of socialists here to understand the historic sources of workers' power. Add to this the unwillingness or inability to defy or change a labor law which, with its restrictions on secondary activity, seems designed to prevent workers from thinking about strategic position and links between unions. Given the historic weakness of the socialist Left—and its recent hopeful resurgence—relaying these insights about the importance of technical and industrial positions, drawn from some of the best organizers the US working class has ever had, is in many ways more urgent now than ever before.

Of course, mechanically applying schemes drawn from the past remains an ever-present danger for a Left prone to looking for cut-and-paste worldviews and solutions. That's why Womack's point about "grubbing" is so important.

By the way, I'm the guy who asked him about strategic positions in telecommunications, as I was trying to write on the leverage unions have in that industry and how it's changing with growth in technology. His answer—"I don't know now. It takes analysis I haven't done"—is refreshing in its honesty and an answer I wish more people would give.

We have to put in the work to discover these strategic positions; it's ongoing, relentless work in the face of capitalist industrial and technical innovation, "a major way capital conducts its struggle with labor," as Womack reminds us. Yet the fundamentals of production under capitalism haven't changed; as Womack says, "Artisans, dirt farmers, proprietary workers might work in isolation. But industrial workers work in cooperation, coordination, simultaneous or sequential or both, maybe in the same productive place or maybe in connection with another somewhere else, near or far." That might look somewhat different today than it did a hundred years ago, but it's important to emphasize the continuity, as well.

I think the bigger context for thinking about Womack's points is that any revival of the US labor movement will require the revival of the strike (and slowdowns, work-to-rule, sit-downs, and other tactics in which workers themselves display their power). We all owe a big debt to the West Virginia teachers for proving this point through, as Womack says, "independent, publicly defiant working-class action."

There's been some useful work published in recent years that has helped spread this argument, such as Jane McAlevey's books, and Joe Burns's *Reviving the Strike* and his new edition *Strike Back: Rediscovering Militant Tactics to Fight the Attacks on Public Employee Unions*, as well as Eric Blanc's *Red-State Revolt*, on the teacher strike wave. We've tried to do our part at *Labor Notes*, covering as many strikes as we can and publishing a pamphlet titled *How to Strike and Win* a couple of years ago.

But any serious revival of the strike will require workers and their organizations to grapple with the questions that Womack raises in this discussion and in his book on strategic position and working-class power. it will mean figuring out which workers are strategically positioned to exert the most leverage, and how to organize them (and convince them to use their power for class-wide, rather than sectional, aims).

The alternative is to continue down the dead-end path of looking for sources of leverage outside of workers themselves. That's not to dismiss that work. Workers absolutely need community and political allies. It's worthwhile to figure out how to leverage pension fund capital and to pressure shareholders—but far too often it's not a complement to but a substitute for workers taking action. The real question is whether we're building a workers' movement or a middle-class advocacy movement where workers are props.[1]

I think the argument that many would make is that thanks to the changes in global capitalism over the past few decades, workers don't have the power, via collective action in the workplace, that they once did, and that we have to reckon with that. But Labor Notes founder Kim Moody has argued that "it usually takes a generation for the workforce to realize the power that it has, and the points of vulnerability."[2] Today, he says, "unions should be able to take advantage of the vulnerable points in just-in-time logistics and production to bring some of these new [corporate] giants to heel."

Womack points in the same direction. "Any product that moves now, anybody who moves, goes through many more connections in chains and networks than a generation ago," he says. Unfortunately, as these connections have multiplied and proliferated across borders, the connections between workers in these chains have not caught up, to say the least. In most cases, what exists are weak ties between staffers from different national union federations and international confederations, rather than the robust ties at the grassroots level that are necessary to launch a coordinated assault.

Though they may be small, there are some developments to be hopeful about, often outside of existing unions. They include the organizing by tech workers at Amazon and Google, organizing which spans borders. These workers often have an intimate knowledge of how the company works, which can help in determining the vulnerable links in the chain and could prove especially useful if they link up with, for example, the groups of Amazon warehouse workers building up workplace committees in a growing number of cities across the country.

Womack's idea about the need for something like a labor institute of industrial technology is intriguing. It would undoubtedly have to be a project of a resurgent socialist Left—maybe some committed labor academics in alliance with a creative, far-thinking set of unions. In the meantime, hopefully this discussion inspires more labor activists—and academics, and labor journalists like myself—to devote more attention to these questions.

No Magic Bullet
Technically Strategic Power Alone Is Not Enough

Katy Fox-Hodess

Building on the work of midcentury American industrial relations scholar and practitioner John T. Dunlop, John Womack argues that strategic positions may be strategic because of the economic, technical, social, cultural, or political role of workers in those positions. However, among these possibilities, Womack is clear that he is primarily concerned with "technically strategic positions," whether within a given workplace, industry, or the economy as a whole. Pointing out that "in Russia in 1917 the Bolsheviks didn't spend effort on organizing shoe-shiners or barbers or bakers or street peddlers or rag pickers," he argues that it is only by focusing on technically strategic positions that workers can "get real leverage over production, the leverage to make their struggle effective. You don't get this leverage just by feelings. You get it by holding the power to cut off the capitalist's revenue. And without that material power your struggle won't get you very far for very long."

In this regard, Womack's conceptualization of technically strategic positions bears striking similarities to the concept of "structural power" developed by Beverly Silver in her 2003 book *Forces of Labor: Workers' Movements and Globalization since 1870*. Examples of workers in

Los Angeles, April 15, 2008: Union members from service employees to longshoremen, to maintenance workers and actors, taking part in a three-day march in the "Hollywood to the Docks" calling for good jobs.
Photo and copyright: Robert Gumpert

technically strategic positions (or, in Silver's formulation, with a high degree of structural power) include workers in heavy manufacturing (i.e., the auto industry) and logistics (i.e., transportation and the ports). Within each sector, certain workers, such as tool and die makers and crane operators, are more technically strategic than others. Whether by sector or job role, the power of technically strategic workers derives from their ability to create disruptive ripples that make waves far beyond their immediate workplace or industry.

Womack's notion of technical relations at work derives from a framework that understands workplaces, industries, and the economy as a whole as webs or networks connected by links that create vulnerabilities that make certain locations far more likely than others to be used as breaking points. As Womack puts it, "In almost every industry… there's no single, complete technology at work… It's always several technologies composed, put together. And wherever you put one thing together with another, there's a seam or a zipper or a hub or a joint or a node or a link, the more technologies together, the more links, the places where it's not integral… and where the parts go together… there can be a bottleneck, a choke point."

Womack is therefore insistent that worker organizers attend to the specifics of the technical vulnerabilities in a given workplace or industry. By careful empirical analysis, Womack argues that these vulnerabilities can be defined objectively in terms of workers' ability to build leverage over capital. The suggestion for the labor movement, then, is to concentrate organizing efforts in the spaces (and times) that will have the greatest impact in terms of disrupting production. Womack's suggestion that these questions can be answered objectively and definitively and that, in doing so, we can maximize our efforts is a compelling one and certainly merits greater consideration by organizers.

On the other hand, Womack is less persuasive on the question of the forms of power available to workers' nontechnical strategic positions and the significance of nontechnical forms of power more generally. Earlier in the interview, he is disparaging of sociologist Erik Olin Wright's concept of "associational power," which refers to forms of power that accrue to workers as a result of their collective organization in trade unions, works councils, and the like.[1] For Womack, associational power at this point in the interview is solely a "derivative power"—"a consequence of strategic power."

Yet, though I began my research on global dockworker trade unionism with a similar perspective to Womack, I've come to the opposite conclusion: strategic power (or structural power) is deeply rooted in associational power.[2] To take a simple illustration of this principle: despite the tremendous strategic potential that dockworkers possess as a result of the technical division of labor in ports and the absolutely central role of ports in global commerce, it turns out that dockworkers do not have powerful unions everywhere around the world. Trade unionism in ports tends to be weak in countries where trade unionism is generally weaker as a result of sociopolitical conditions. That is to say, the lack of associational power available to these workers precludes the possibility of them exercising strategic power effectively, or in many cases, at all. For example, in Colombia, dockworkers historically had a powerful national union. But their union was destroyed overnight when the country's ports were privatized in the early 1990s. Three decades later, they continue to struggle for basic union recognition, as dockworkers' strategic position does not exempt them from the extremely adverse conditions for trade unionism in general in the most dangerous country in the world for trade unionists.[3]

Womack is prepared to concede that associational

power does matter, "however derivative it is," in crisis situations when "you've got to have many people for your struggle, your cause, morally, politically." He suggests that "if it comes as a total surprise… everybody else in the country is against it" and that new replacements, either "civilian" or "military" could be found for striking workers within the week. The problem, however, is that Womack's laser-like focus on the technical division of labor doesn't allow him to provide a comprehensive explanation of why broad-based support seems to matter quite a bit for strategically positioned workers at certain moments. My research on dockworkers, however, suggests that broad-based social support for this highly (technically) strategic group of workers is critical to maintaining their ability to exercise technical strategic power in the first place. In Portugal, for example, dockworkers faced down an attempt to subject their union-controlled labor pools to nonunion competition—one of the terms of the Portuguese state's bailout agreement following the sovereign debt crisis. While the dockworkers were able to effectively leverage their strategic position through targeted strike action—and the threat of a boycott of ships leaving Lisbon by dockworkers in Spain—union leaders emphasized the importance of the large coalition they built with many nonstrategic workers, including the unemployed, who helped to amplify the dockworkers' message that their struggle was in the interests of Portuguese workers as a whole. Taken together, these forms of technically strategic pressure at the point of production and sociopolitical pressure through broad-based coalitions enabled a major victory in this phase of the Portuguese dockworkers' struggle.[4]

The necessity of broad-based support is not incidental but instead intrinsic to their technically strategic position. Because technically strategic workers have the power to send disruptive ripples far beyond their immediate workplaces, they find themselves in conflict with both capital and the capitalist state again and again. The ripple effects of disruptions through industrial action tend to reach multiple sectors of capital as well as other workers—for example, the transportation strikes that shut down the evening commute or result in scarcities of basic commodities—creating a reiterative threat that "public opinion" may turn against the highly strategic striking workers. In such cases, when public opinion turns, it is far easier for the state to move against workers in a repressive capacity. In other words, *the strongest position from a technically strategic perspective may simultaneously be the weakest position from a social or political perspective, with important consequences for labor strategy.*

As a result, deep-rooted alliances and shared understandings with less technically strategically positioned workers and other groups in society may serve as an effective buffer against overly repressive measures by the state as it weighs the possibility of a crisis of profitability, driven by strategically positioned workers withholding their labor, against the possibility of a crisis of legitimacy if the state represses union action. In other words, creating and maintaining a buffer through building long-term, mutually beneficial links with workers who have a weaker degree of technically strategic power, but a high degree of social or political strategic power, ups the stakes of repressive state intervention, making it more likely for technically strategically positioned workers to succeed through industrial action. The crucial point here, contra Womack, is that technically strategically privileged workers require the social and political power of less technically strategically privileged workers (and other actors in civil society) just as much as the latter require the technical power of the former.

The power of these alliances was on full display in strikes in recent years by dockworkers in Chile, who have built surprisingly strong relationships with the student movement—for many years, the strongest social movement in the country. Student activists provided myriad forms of support to the dockworkers, including building linkages throughout the country and amplifying the dockworkers' message, as in the case with the unemployed workers' support for the Portuguese dockworkers. This proved especially important in countering negative coverage of the strike in the media and raising the stakes of further state repression after arrests and beatings on the picket lines. The dockworkers reciprocated with solidarity strikes for the students, and the coalition has endured over time as they have worked together to redress the enduring inequalities and democratic deficits in the country that have remained since the Pinochet dictatorship.

In sum, power flows in multiple directions across multiple dimensions—economic, social, and political—in conflicts between capital and labor. The more strategic the industry, the more likely it is that the capitalist state will intervene. As a result, labor movement revitalization will require understanding not only how to find and take advantage of vulnerabilities in the technical division of labor but also how to find and take advantages of economic, social, and political vulnerabilities within the capitalist totality. This will by necessity require a clear understanding of the forms of power each group of workers may offer and a clear understanding that success will come through *articulating and combining* powers across multiple dimensions, suggesting the need to rethink hierarchies that privilege the technical over the social and political.

Aliquippa, Pennsylvania 1986: LTV closed Aliquippa Steel Works. Idled rail cars once carried raw material for the steel process but are no longer needed. Photo and copyright: Robert Gumpert

Organizing Strategic Workers on "the Seam"

A Response to the "Foundry Interviews" with John Womack Jr.

Carey Dall

> "Wherever things connect, that's where they're materially weakest, maybe politically, legally, commercially, culturally strong, protected, defended, but technically weakest. Follow the admirable Peter Roth's principle: 'If you build it, it can fail.' ... It's hard to tear fabric woven whole, like Christ's cloak, all of one piece; it's much easier to tear it where there's a seam." (26)

"If you build it, it can fail." Students of American labor history know this only too well. Happily, the same can be said of capitalist entities, providing endless opportunities for American workers to radically transform their political, economic, and social conditions in the US and, by extension, everywhere else.

The price of revolutionary progress is we must think and act strategically. Womack, in discussion with Perušek and Olney, reminds us that moral certainty and willingness to be militant are not enough. We must seek out the Womackian "seams" and then organize well to empower workers to exploit capital's weaknesses at these seams.

For every example of strategic organizing along Womackian seams, our labor movement has too many examples of struggling to tear Christ's cloak: Attempts to organize Walmart workers and the Fight for $15 are two such commendable efforts to raise up the most oppressed among us. But these struggles fail fundamentally to broadly achieve their stated goals because they refuse to identify the weak links in their targets' profitability. Identifying and exacerbating those weaknesses definitively involves workers at a handful of points of production and cannot be substituted by the "air war" of communications strategies, legislative meanderings, and lawsuits. A comprehensive strategy involving all the above with the help of the surrounding "community" is ideal.

With a respectful nod to the all-important work of organizing new union members in strategic positions, let us consider the vital work of *reorganizing* union members in the United States. Comprehensive "internal organizing," like high-impact research, should never stop. By the middle of the twentieth century, too many unions traded strategic and militant action for business unionism. Our resulting labor history is a carnage pile of ill-equipped workers and myopic union leaders being mauled by better resourced and rapaciously antihuman capitalists.[1] Whereas capitalists have studied *our* seams and acted accordingly, we have generally studied very little and relied on bargaining table prowess and "air wars" to deliver the goods. The goods have yet to materialize.

Internal organizing begins with the assumption that to make lasting transformations, workers need to be totally involved in a transparent struggle. This is badly needed throughout the entire labor movement, but here I will focus on transportation, which is where I have organized for the past twenty years. Multidimensional seams exist in the transmission of cargo from one node to another, as in rail to truck or rail to ship. These can be exploited toward societally transformative ends. It helps that whereas overall union density in the US is now at an all-time low, strategically vital transportation subsectors such as longshore[2] and rail[3] are roughly 85 percent union.

The workers in these unions are not internally organized in a way that can use their strategic position to make deep changes in the society.[4] For starters, the leaders of rail and longshore unions do not collaborate. Furthermore, the workers of different rail crafts are spatially and culturally isolated from each other, and from longshore workers. Except for the internal organizing program at the Brotherhood of Maintenance of Way (BMWED-IBT), which I directed from 2015 through early 2021, no recent attempt has been made in any of these unions to empower the members at the points of production to wield their economic power for self-interest, not to mention societal interest.

The Womackian seam in this world is where the railroads intersect with the waterfront terminals. The workers at these strategic nodes are almost all unionized, and mostly free from the paralyzing fear that nonunion workers without contractual protections rightfully feel. Capital is relatively weak in this space for the moment. With the loud march of automation, this will not always be the case—but as Womack reminds us, even the robots are vulnerable![5]

Strategic internal organizing faces many headwinds. I will focus on three.

First, of the rail and longshore unions only the ILWU ever had hard cores of leftist, revolutionary cadres throughout its geographic jurisdiction.[6] These have largely receded into history, leaving behind a reflexive progressivism without any strategic foundation. The other unions—the International Longshoremen's Association and rail labor—were born as craft-specific "brotherhoods" whose leaders actively repelled industrial unionism (for rail, in the form of the American Railway Union led by Eugene V. Debs), and left-wing cadre organization wherever it gained a foothold. Without left-wing organizers pushing radical analysis and strategic direct action throughout the memberships, leadership has generally been collaborative with capital with few notable exceptions.

The second headwind is the members themselves. If we look at members of these unions in the current period, their condition and where many (but not all) find themselves geographically are significant obstacles for deep internal organizing. During the age of Trump, many rail workers responded to the massive vacuum of leadership and education in their unions by defying leaders' political endorsements and supporting the xenophobia, racism, and warmongering of the clownish billionaire. The members of my union, the BMWED, are intentionally hired from the interior and countryside by railroads fearful of the "resistant nature" of inner-city workers. Contradictions abound when rural dirt farmers, whose political education happens in the deer stand or on right-wing social media—far away from the fiery urban trade unionism of the ILWU—find themselves struggling to make sense of a highly capitalized industry responsible for the movement of the nation's cargo. When unions throw up their hands and give up in the face of this contradiction, we all lose.

The third headwind is derivative of the first two: our unions lack the capacity to take comprehensive advantage of the seams. This is not natural. It is the result of the objective societal forces swirling around us in combination with a severe leadership vacuum at virtually every level of our unions. Strong leaders will target resources at the development of members' analytical and organizing skills, all at the expense of the labor bureaucrats hell-bent on hiding behind the desk preparing arbitrations. This precious internal organizing is happening in a handful of spaces, resulting in breathtaking struggles that are reviving the radical imagination in the US. Such intentional, transformative efforts are taking place among unionized teachers (especially in Chicago and Los Angeles), airline workers (Association of Flight Attendants–Communication Workers of America), and nurses (National Nurses United).

To take on Amazon and other threats in the transportation sector, unions will have to overcome the three headwinds that I discuss. To organize Amazon workers, we must first internally organize union transportation workers whose labor on the seams enables Amazon to get cargo of Asian origin to their hellish warehouses and finally to the consumer's door. Our existence as a labor movement depends on this. The hour is getting late.

Long Beach, 1983: A striking Greyhound worker and son at a rally for several striking unions. Photo and copyright: Robert Gumpert

Associational Power, Too

Jack Metzgar

John Womack's insistent focus on finding strategic worker positions within webs of production, whether an entire economy or a single workplace, is well taken. And his vast knowledge of different work processes in different countries at different periods fruitfully illustrates the complexity of the kind of ongoing systems analysis he calls for in union organizing. But he is too given to posing either/ors where there are dialectics, and this causes him to miss the impracticality of focusing strictly on strategic positions that can upend capitalist power relations.

This comes out clearly in his dismissal of "associational power" as secondary and derivative of "structural power." (31–32) Associational power is about solidarity among workers and with the broader public and the willingness to act in association to change circumstances, whether you have structural power or not. For Womack, only "material power in action, the force of leverage over production moving great weight against profit… can lead workers in hope and courage to associate and go forward, appealing to popular morality or indignation" (31). This greatly underestimates the importance of solidarity, associational power, in both nonstrategic and strategic positions.

First, workers often have the "hope and courage to associate and go forward" even when they might have little chance of effecting change. Are union organizers supposed to warn such workers against this folly or attempt to direct their hope and courage in the most fruitful direction possible in a given situation? That's a hard choice many organizers must make, not one that has a ready answer related to how strategic a group of workers happens to be. When people are ready to move, to challenge authority and present their grievances, they need to carefully assess the potential risks and benefits of such action, but they cannot be counseled to simply give up because they are not strategic. Besides, no organizer is wise enough to know when sheer associational power can win something important to workers, how this might spur future organizing to build even stronger associational power, and then where that additional power might lead.

Womack cites the 1919 steel strike as an instance where the lead organizer, William Z. Foster, had a clear-headed sense of the steel industry's strategic position immediately after World War I. But that strike was lost when thousands did not strike and then when thousands crossed their own picket lines. Steelworkers in 1919 had numerous divisions among them, most importantly by skill and by race and ethnicity. They had insufficient associational power to take advantage of their structural power and strategic position. Womack is right to see how associational power can derive from structural power, but it doesn't always and certainly not automatically. And when it doesn't, even the most strategic position cannot hold.

When asked about recent teachers' strikes in West Virginia and Oklahoma, Womack seems to give central importance to associational power—"that culture of resistance and rebellion… bred [into] children and grand-children, steeped in organizing to fight for their causes.

(54). He does note that teachers have "a special socially strategic position" because they can "disrupt the social lives of every family with children in the state" (55). The experience of the Chicago Teachers Union, for example, who struck again in 2019, suggests that careful attention to building associational power with parents is crucial to winning teachers' strikes. That power to disrupt families is a double-edged sword that cuts against teachers when parents are either hostile or indifferent. Chicago teachers got good raises, but they struck on issues of class size, increased wraparound services, and even affordable housing that were important to parents as well as teachers. Even in Womack's account of teachers, it looks like it was associational power that built teachers' strategic position, not the other way around.

Strategic position *is* as important as Womack claims but is not the only important thing. Nonstrategic workers, like those in retail and personal care, need to organize and form unions too. Nonstrategic workers already in unions, like hotel and restaurant workers, need to organize themselves to win better wages and conditions and so they can organize others. Unions always have limited resources, especially now, and that's why they need to focus their organizing, as Womack argues, on workers in strategic positions that can win power not only for themselves but for other workers and for the working class as a whole. But all forms of organizing are about building associational power, solidarity, the power of numbers in organized collective action. Associational power is necessary (and not derivative) to turn technically strategic positions into powerful economic and political levers that can bend capital to the popular will.

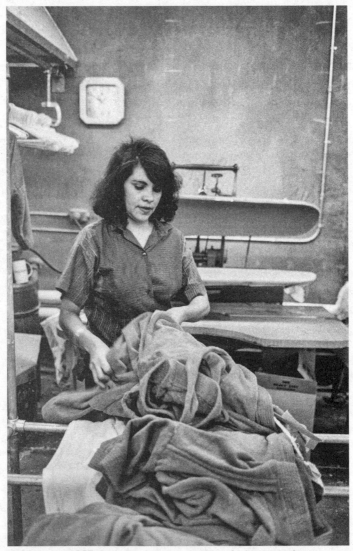

Los Angeles, 1987: A presser in a garment shop in downtown Los Angeles. Photo and copyright: Robert Gumpert

An Opinion in the Context of the "Foundry Interviews"

Joel Ochoa

▬▬▬▬▬▬

I first encountered the work of John Womack in 1971, when one of my professors gave me a copy of *Zapata and the Mexican Revolution*. As a young activist in Mexico City, inspired by the revolutionary fervor of the time, I found the book provocative. It challenged me to recognize the relationship between Zapata, the Mexican revolutionary, and his own immediate base. Zapata was elected by the elders of his community to continue the fight for their own survival.

This Womack interview comes at an ambivalent time, because there are plenty of reasons why we, collectively, can be both encouraged and concerned. Mass mobilizations in various parts of the world grappling with different issues are demanding an end to the policies first established on a world scale during the Reagan/Thatcher era. They give hope because of the possibility of change. Yet given the absence of a clearly elaborated response, especially from the Left, concern emerges because it is hard to see the kind of change that inevitably will be necessary.

Womack speaks of the need for a strategic approach to the revival of one of the principal targets of neoliberal policies: organized labor. And his analysis on this subject is, at least, illustrative. Given the polarization created worldwide during the last thirty years, however, we have to realize that labor, at the moment, only represents one of the victims.

The weakening of the state gave way to the decline of regulations; this, in turn, facilitated the process of casualization of labor and left the environment unprotected. Facing a loss of revenue due to unfair tax policies and an unregulated banking system, the state lost the capacity to sustain, according to the needs of the population, social programs such as health, education, and food, among others. Without protection at home and facing fierce competition on a global scale, workers from developed countries were displaced. This outcome was determined by market forces and was bleak.

Globalization and the integration of computers into production processes paved the way for the elimination of jobs that at one time were considered strategic. What once was called the "labor aristocracy" almost disappeared as a result of mechanization, or simply because those jobs were packaged as part of some sort of trade agreement. The leverage created with the passage of the National Labor Relations Act (NLRA) and its radical implementation, especially by the Congress of Industrial Organizations, is almost nonexistent, to the point where we keep losing vital benefits like pensions, wages, and medical coverage. Organized labor as a whole appears unable to marshal the solidarity necessary to stop the bleeding.

Labor and workers in general face daunting challenges. The effects of what Womack identifies as "vertical disintegration" (the end of Fordism?) is part of our daily life and the fate of auto workers. It presents a classical example of how an important industry was fragmented and greatly changed. A symptom of that transformation is the current state of the United Automobile Workers (UAW) in the United States; once considered a vanguard in the negotiation of benefits for its members, the union has been fundamentally weakened and is incapable of bargaining without resort to crippling concessions.

Here is the rub, at least the way I see it: organized labor must seriously look into the issue of solidarity, from within and also externally. It will be mutually beneficial for labor, as an institution, and the different components of the accumulation of forces, worldwide, currently fighting the catastrophic effects of neoliberalism, to find real points of convergence and cooperation. Organized labor can create momentum by organizing in nonstrategic sectors. This needs to be done using a programmatic and sustained approach. If unions take this avenue, they will be bringing more women and minorities into their ranks; and in both cases, we are talking about the future of unions. Furthermore, these sectors have shown an incredible capacity to mobilize and support other causes. This could pave the way for unions to form alliances with environmentalists, women's groups, youth, and minorities. In all of this, the issue of solidarity and working with minorities is only natural, especially if we consider that regardless of different approaches, we all face the same enemy.

The experience in Southern California over the last forty-plus years illustrates this point.

The Los Angeles County Federation of Labor is the second largest central labor council in the United States. It is also one of the most progressive and inclusive. The vibrancy of the members whose unions are affiliated to the LA County Fed has helped to mold the kind of progressive politics we enjoy in Southern California. But it wasn't always like this. In the 1970s, one union in particular made some radical changes in their approach to organizing. The International Ladies' Garment Workers' Union (ILGWU), a union hardly considered "strategic" in the industrial sector, created alliances, especially with Asian and Latino community-based organizations, and paved the way for many of the changes we currently enjoy. For instance, they negotiated language into their contracts protecting the undocumented, they hired activists and workers from within to be organizers, and eventually their leadership became Latino and women, reflecting the workforce.

It is safe to say that the ILGWU was a life changer for immigrant workers. It paved the way for the implementation of the Immigration Reform and Control Act of 1986 signed into law by Ronald Reagan, after which more than three million immigrants applied for legal status. This empowering act, the legalization, combined with the militancy of Latino immigrants resulted in two important successes: (1) Workers joining unions at a considerable scale, top down and bottom up, in different industrial sectors such as Justice for Janitors in service, American Racing Equipment in manufacturing, and drywall carpenters in residential construction. (2) The mass participation in the fight against the anti-immigrant Proposition 187. The former gave way to a more powerful labor movement; the latter changed the face of politics in California.

When I first read Womack's *Zapata*, I recall the Mexican revolutionary preparing to fight the excesses of the liberal policies of the time. Years later, another book of his, this time about the uprising in my home state of Chiapas, Mexico, of the indigenous EZLN (Ejército Zapatista de Liberación Nacional), centered on the fight that was, and still is, against the neoliberal policies of the North American Free Trade Agreement signed by presidents Clinton and Salinas. Now I have another reference point for my respect and reverence for Womack in reading his thoughtful deliberations on working-class strategy and power. Viva Womack!

Who Will Lead the Campaign?

Rand Wilson

━━━━━━━━━

Jack Womack's insights on the role of strategic workers in the production process directly build on Harry Braverman's seminal book, *Labor and Monopoly Capital: The Degradation of Work in the Twentieth Century*.[1] A book that "literally christened the emerging field of labor process studies" and that in turn "reinvigorated intellectual sensibilities and revived the study of the work process in fields such as history, sociology, economics, political science, and human geography."[2] In my youth, Braverman's ideas about the labor process resonated with my personal experience working at different jobs and strongly influenced me to pursue organizing at the point of production.

His work, as brilliant as it was, mainly focused on Taylorism and management's control of workers and the labor process. What is especially exciting about Womack's work is it takes us on *the offensive* with strategies for workers to gain power. In particular, I like his thinking about management's weakness during periods of transition. Womack recognizes that when the bosses introduce new technology or reorganize the labor process, it creates a special vulnerable moment—and a new window of opportunity for workers.

San Francisco, 1983: A paint foreman directs his crew near the top of the north tower of the Golden Gate Bridge. Photo and copyright: Robert Gumpert

Womack urges us to gain more knowledge about who is a strategic worker and where the key choke points might be in an employer's work process. He calls for increased research and even speculates about the need for a new institute or college devoted to such studies. Certainly the labor movement needs institutions devoted to assisting our on-the-ground organizing. After all, the business class has legions of researchers, technicians, and human relations "experts" training managers to strengthen the hand of capital.

In my experience as an organizer, however, we gain knowledge about strategic workers, choke points, and leverage organically from the workers engaged in the union building process or from union leaders during the contract campaign. Workers are almost always the most knowledgeable source of information about who is in the best position to disrupt the production process or services and where management's weaknesses lie. Even better, once their knowledge is distilled into a coherent battle plan, they own the results and gain confidence to implement it. No PhDs needed.

One major weakness of US labor law is that often the most strategic workers are intentionally excluded from the union's defined bargaining unit. For example, it's a constant struggle in the organizing process to include the IT department where many of today's most strategic workers are located. Management opposes it during the formation of unions; and as often as not, the IT workers are a well-taken-care-of elite who aren't interested. In many firms, highly skilled technicians and programmers are subcontracted to an outside company.

Identifying strategic workers is all well and good, but shop floor leaders willing to take action are equally important when seeking to realize labor's potential power in the workplace. Thus it's often the case that the union's best course forward is with those members ready to lead, even if not in the most powerful position to do so.

Building workers' confidence in their union requires a mix of smart strategies informed by Womack's methods of strategic research and a long-term investment in workers inspired to be leaders of their own collective destiny.

How to Read Womack

Jane McAlevey

John Womack hammers home two key points that deserve urgent attention today. One is dependent upon the other. First, the ongoing need to research, analyze, and study the choke points in specific workplaces, the sector in which they exist, and the economy overall. Second, with that analysis, a persistent awareness that if broad swaths of society are not organized around and in support of the workers at the heart of key choke points, even technically strategic workers will likely fail. In support of these core concepts, he spells out his message repeatedly: "But unless you have the power of disruption, you can't realistically develop any strategic plan, extended or limited" (39). His clarity about "power of disruption"—is welcome. Anyone who has been fortunate enough to win positive, substantial structural change through collective action understands the difference between the rhetoric of the 99 percent and the reality of what it takes to forge unity and structure among the 99 percent!

What leaves me wanting for more from Womack's work, however, is the discussion of the workers with technical or positional power (mostly referred to as technical, in the sense of train dispatchers rather than rail workers who

San Francisco, 1994: Housecleaner, a member of the Hotel and Restaurant Employees Local 2, cleans a bathroom at one of San Francisco's higher-end hotels. Photo and copyright: Robert Gumpert

sell tickets) and workers with what he calls social power. For organizers in the United States and much of Europe—where the process of deindustrialization, combined with deunionization, has produced a working class that rarely identifies as working class—the challenge of identifying where capitalists are vulnerable to a crisis generated by working-class power seems to require a further blurring of what Womack refers to as "material power." For example, Womack says,

> In a crisis you've got to have many people for your struggle, your cause, morally, politically, and that's association, people encouraged, heartened, emboldened by material power in action for them, but moved, mobilized, by appeals in civil society to interest or justice, or both. But without material power in action, real force, all you get is association in action, movements, which in their heyday may be inspiring, but continually, always fade. *Only with material power—not with it only, but only with it, on its strength—can you force change and keep it* (32).

The nagging question of what constitutes material power looms large. As the interview nears its end, Womack reflects on the recent education strikes in West Virginia and in his birthplace, Oklahoma, saying: "Those teachers, as they threatened to disrupt the social lives of every family with children in the state, quickly caught public attention. It was in public action that they made the public recognize how miserable their salaries were, how vicious the threats to their benefits were."

Understanding that public, collective action won the day is, it seems, 100 percent accurate. But was the strike by educators disrupting only "the social lives of every family," or are massive strikes in two key sectors of today's economy—education and health care (each heavily reliant on taxpayer funding)—actually strikes with "material power" too? This question and the broader questions of where the greatest success can be generated—by which kind of disruptive action, by which people, in which economic sector, and in which geography—are of central importance today.

Womack points us in all useful directions. But the issue of actions in the so-called private sector (where capitalists profits are more centrally challenged) versus actions in the so-called public sector (which seem to be theorized here as more of social power) is unresolved. And perhaps for good reason: it is complex. For example, in West Virginia, the education sector is the first- or second-largest employer in almost every county. More often than not, it's the largest employer. And while shutting down schools and the people who shut them down—educators—are seen as causing a social crisis, it's hard to argue that if the education sector is the largest employer, and if the breadwinner in most homes today is likely to be a woman in the public sector and not a man in the private sector, then the question of what constitutes material power is underdeveloped or perhaps not thoroughly theorized.

From an organizer's viewpoint, the question is, are the workers capable of creating a crisis big enough that it forces the employers to make concessions? We know the owners and shareholders at the very top don't sort the "public" and "private" sector the way we do but rather own it all and use the public sector as their personal piggy bank, extracting as much value as they can from both. So isn't the definition of "material power" far more fluid? It took four days of a 100 percent out strike in Los Angeles for the mayor and the state's governor to intervene and help find a solution because six hundred thousand kids out of the classroom is more than a "social power" crisis, it's also an economic crisis at that scale. (It took two more full days of the 100 percent out strike before a settlement was reached.) In my own experiences, mostly grounded in the cases of health-care workers, it can take less time, only a day or two, if, say, key hospital emergency departments in a major city are all in crisis from a multi-employer strike, while nursing home workers might require a week or more to create the same level of crisis.

In the first hospital strikes waged in Las Vegas, in 2006, after just two days on the picket lines, the entire political elite of the state, from the Democratic mayor to the Democratic speaker of the house to the Republican governor, intervened to create enough leverage to demand a solution to the "crisis." In a telling moment of the nuances even among service workers, the then leader of the mighty Culinary Workers Local 226 (and now president of the national union), D. Taylor, walked into an emergency meeting of the striking nurses and declared, "Casino workers have to go on strike for years before they generate the attention and power you just did in 48 hours!"

The two central points of this very smart John Womack interview—that we have to be vigorous in our research and analysis and that we have to be able to unearth strategic disruption—are absolutely as true today as they were 50 years ago in the black freedom movement, which he mentions, and 80 years ago in the sit-down strikes, and 125 years ago in railway and other strikes covered in this rich discussion. Underexplored and urgently needed is more discussion about how to create a crisis that forces the political elite to make real, tangible concessions to the working class. Clearly, it is theoretically possible to organize the workers who could stop the two-day guaranteed delivery of billionaire Bezos's Amazon Prime. But to soften the terrain to make organizing possible against his unlawful, immoral behavior, the workers today in the best position to move strategic power—more than merely "social power"—are the health-care workers and educators who for the time being remain together, side by side, in structured workplaces, throughout every community in every political geography.

Although not at all dismissed by Womack in this interview, the use of the term "social power" for strikes by workers in the two most stable parts of the economy in the US and much of the Global North—education and health care—undervalues the economic power of the women leading the most dynamically successful strikes in the past three decades. The sooner the labor movement, and the broader movement, understands the strategic power of mostly women workers as all-encompassing economic, social, cultural, and political, the faster we get to creating the conditions to tackle the unorganized logistics sector. This seems obvious: as Womack himself stresses in his interview, it's when public, collective action is taken that other workers will be more likely to act. But the gendered bias that power is best exercised by mostly men in the dated conception of the male-dominant private sector, where "material power" can be forged, needs serious reconsideration. In a deunionized country, the women, often if not mostly women of color, forging the biggest strikes in decades, are exercising strategic power that deftly harnesses economic and social power that can't be easily pulled apart.

Read Womack, do power structure analysis, look at which workers are causing the biggest crises for the political elite—and consider women in the public sector as today's most powerful actors in wielding working-class power that demands universal, societal demands not merely for a good union contract but for a changed world.

Abandon the Banking Method!
To Build Solidarity, We Must Practice a Liberatory Pedagogy

Melissa Shetler

I came to both the labor movement and academic scholarship late in life, but I have been a worker, in many sectors, and an educator and facilitator for much of my life. For this reason, I was particularly struck by John Womack's thoughts on sectors of work and strategic positioning. By studying a field of work and points of production, he observes, one can figure out how to strategically disrupt production. In the current environment, however—characterized by globalization, rapid change, the constantly adaptive nature of work, and our need to tie the labor movement back to a struggle of economic justice for all—truly effective interventions must start with worker education. And that education must be participatory.

As a teacher and a unionist, I am most interested in how we practice education that is a cycle of learning and dialogue, that engenders hope and curiosity, and that builds workers' power. Identifying strategic hubs or nodes where the threat of a strike is dangerous to a company's bottom line is important. But, as Womack points out, such moves will always be met with countermoves by capital. Whatever your strategy, creating the conditions, and building readiness, for effective action is critical. The essence of

The Bay Bridge, between San Francisco and Oakland, 2001: Bay Bridge
painter and member of International Union of Painters and Allied Trades.
Photo and copyright: Robert Gumpert

this is in finding ways to engender solidarity and to foster working-class consciousness.

"Education" is often presented as a solution, even as the education of organizers, leaders, and members is woefully underfunded and underwhelming in many unions. But, to my mind, the primary problem isn't the lack of investment in educating our members, or even a "strategic" education. Instead, the key problem is the overwhelming tendency to employ the kind of education that was created with the goal of encouraging passivity and making compliant factory workers. Applying the tools of capitalism to the task of resisting capitalism can be like trying to build a wall with a mining drill. Using what the great Brazilian educator Paolo Freire called the "banking" method of education fails to liberate members.[1] To think strategically, union members must learn to identify and interrogate the assumptions of the status quo. Union pedagogy—like all effective pedagogy—should inculcate both the skills of critical thinking and a vision of the student and worker as both the learner *and* the knower. To achieve this, we need nothing less than a revolution in how we educate members. Leadership will need to rethink their ideas around education, and to be willing to learn "with" and not "over" their membership. And workers will need time to acclimate to a newer model. Using the tools of popular education—looking to change social structures through critical reflection and action—is a step in the right direction.

In a prior role, as director of organizing at a large New York City construction union, I taught campaign strategy and sought to build an internal organizing team. In the process, I directly observed how popular education can illuminate new, better, and more inclusive pathways to power. Leadership expected me to submit a lesson plan detailing exactly what would be taught, an approach that would have undermined the ability to work from the experience of individuals in the class—and union members in the classes, accustomed to the banking method, vocalized a skepticism encapsulated in the question: "If there isn't an expert in this room, why am I wasting my time?" But over time they also saw firsthand the magic that can happen when you trust the process and truly work from what Freire called "generative themes." When we allow workers to take on the action and the reflection, through a dialogue that is respectful of their doubts, participants become the actors in their own struggle and the agents of their own education. Their empowerment is part of it, and uncomfortable moments are part of it. As an educator, to navigate the process successfully you have to really believe that to build worker power, you have to empower groups and individuals and watch it unfold—it's not just amassing individuals who agree. They have to feel their agency. Critical-consciousness-raising education is messy, in a sense. It doesn't look like the traditional models to which we have grown accustomed, which may serve well when transferring technical skills, but not for organizing.

From my own experience in union and other classrooms, I know that letting go of the ego is truly difficult. As the "teacher," you're expected to be the expert in the room, and you take a big risk when you model not superior knowledge and mastery but open dialogue and curiosity. But I've also found that entering a relationship of colearning, rather than "being the teacher," is the beginning of building trust. (Of course this approach still requires rigorous preparation. Colearning doesn't mean winging it; quite the opposite!) But shifting the focus from *transferring knowledge* to facilitating *learning together* can be transformative.

Doing so helps people recognize and unearth their own innate knowledge and talents. In this model, workers' lived, on-the-job experience becomes critical, as it should: They know their workplace, they know the culture, they know the struggles, and they often know or can come up with solutions that are much more relevant than a facilitator could. By contrast, teaching them to recite the history of the National Labor Relations Act and the NLRB does little to build power or to educate members. That is not to say that such history is irrelevant. It importantly contextualizes current struggles and should be taught. But it is the method of teaching that is the critical thing. I've sat through a number of "organizer trainings" in which I spent days being talked at. I watched as those around me struggled to stay engaged. We were told that learning to listen was the most important skill an organizer could have, yet no one was modelling listening. Instead, the expert stood at the front of the room and lectured to the class, occasionally reading slides from a PowerPoint, until we had all been "filled" with information and sent back to "organize." With this approach, it isn't hard to see why members often remain apathetic.

If we want an activated membership, we must practice a participatory democracy, and a participatory pedagogy, that will engage them. To develop leaders, or even better recognize and support already existing ones, we must engage workers in collective action in which they are valued, heard, and able to leverage their power. While identifying strategic choke points can indeed be effective, what was strategic today may not be strategic tomorrow. Without a broad analysis, organizers can spend all their time building power around a position that, in a swiftly evolving global economy, suddenly no longer exists. But if we build broader power, learn to be adaptive, and practice participatory democracy, we can construct new ways of being within the old structures that may ultimately generate momentum. Doing so may reveal that people in all positions have the potential to exert leverage. We must not overlook the possibility that building such solidarity can send shockwaves from the bottom to the top. When an Amazon executive walked off the job recently to protest the firing of whistleblowers who spoke up about condi-tions inside the company's warehouses, it made headlines. With broader empowerment among workers and a greater sense of identification across organizational hierarchies, such action might even become commonplace. There are exciting examples of this pedagogy being engaged, from literacy and ESL projects with garment workers in Alberta, Canada,[2] to the broad approaches outlined in *Teaching for Change: Popular Education and the Labor Movement*.[3]

In the end, I believe that successful pedagogy—and successful labor organizing—is community building. It is engaging in a dialogue that helps us to better understand our own positions, and that of others, and to question the assumptions we may be making about different groups or values. It's sharing stories, it's listening deeply, it's being willing to be uncomfortable enough to learn something new and engage in truly transformative learning.[4] This, I believe, is what builds solidarity, empowers workers, and generates lasting leverage. This is what creates a movement.

Thirty-Two Thousand Hogs and Not a Drop to Drink

Gene Bruskin

The hogs begin arriving at the Smithfield, North Carolina, plant in trucks by the hundreds and then by the thousands, starting at 6:00 a.m. By the end of each day, thirty-two thousand hogs are delivered, six days a week. They thunder off the trucks—275 pounds, strong, and crazed—after spending most of their eight-months-long lives penned up in cages barely large enough to allow them to breathe. The ninety workers in the livestock department are charged with funneling them through an ever-smaller series of interlocking pens, eventually leading to a "gas chamber" where they are gassed, lowered one floor down in the chamber, unconscious, and dumped down a chute onto the kill floor.

As the hogs do not march in an orderly follow-the-leader line when they are herded off the trucks, workers are forced to be inside the pens guiding them through the various gates. It was not unusual for workers to get knocked down by the hogs and then pulled off to safety by their coworkers, only to have management ignore their reports of these incidents. A key insight happens for workers when they come on the job in livestock: "They care more about the hogs than the people."

Central Valley, California 2003: A worker boxes up tomatoes at a central distribution center near Sacramento. Photo and copyright: Robert Gumpert

At the bottom of the chute to the kill floor, the hogs are shackled and hooked onto a chain that lifts them and attaches them to an overhead conveyor belt to carry them through the kill floor, where their throats are slit. The draining blood, like every ounce of the hog, is captured and sold. Smithfield likes to brag that they control the entire process, "from the squeal to the meal." From there they are cut into many pieces and, after spending the night in cold storage, are processed as ham or other pork products, packaged, and loaded into trucks to begin the trip to supermarkets across the country and as far away as China and Japan. (WH Group, a Chinese company, purchased Smithfield in 2013.)

In December 2005, the United Food and Commercial Workers union asked me to direct the Justice@Smithfield Campaign. The effort to organize the five thousand workers at Smithfield's Tar Heel, North Carolina, plant—the world largest slaughterhouse—had begun when the plant opened in 1992. Many of Smithfield's operations across the country were unionized before being acquired by Smithfield, and the union remained in those locations. But the company was determined to keep the Tar Heel plant, where up to 40 percent of its hogs would be processed, nonunion.

The union lost two NLRB elections in the 1990s when Smithfield, the world's largest multinational pork processor, committed rampant unfair labor practices (ULPs). The ULPs were still crawling through the courts when I came onboard. The union had finally given up on the legal strategy for bringing the workers justice; they decided to run an all-out campaign to bring Smithfield to the table either to agree on card check or to negotiate favorable terms for a fair election.

Although I had many years of organizing experience at that time, I had never tackled the meatpacking industry and certainly had not run a campaign in an area as large and as rural as southeastern North Carolina. Most unfortunately, I had not read John Womack.

In retrospect, some of his insights describe the strategies we eventually came to in order to gain leverage in this David-and-Goliath struggle with a corporation run by an ideologically driven CEO, the son of the company's founder. To say the least, it was an imposing challenge.

Womack brilliantly explains some of our not-so-articulated approaches:

- Find the best link to break; wherever things connect, that's where they're materially weakest.
- Measure the damage that you can do with the backing you have and the benefits that you can gain.
- Determine how much the workers want to interrupt and disrupt, how far and for how long.
- Use "associative power" to back up your "strategic power" at the choke points. In this case it was our market-based community campaign.
- Determine how to efficiently impact revenue.

In our approach, the Justice@Smithfield Campaign created an inside/outside strategy.

- Disrupt production and the smooth flow of plant operations in as many ways as possible through worker actions.
- Focus internally and externally on the unsafe and even brutal conditions the workers faced day to day.
- Build a field campaign that involves consumers, shareholders, religious organizations, labor, and media and is based in community engagement, for example the message that Smithfield's products were "packaged with abuse" that workers themselves delivered to the public.

- Bring the broad public support we can build behind the worker actions into the plant to protect the workers from retaliation.

After hearing about the almost indescribable conditions inside the plant, I was convinced that this was the right strategy. Remarkably, after all these years, once the workers believed we knew what we were doing, and that we would listen to and include them and, importantly, would back them, they stepped forward again. But this still did not get to Womack's concept of choke points.

Despite the huge turnover, we mapped the massive plant extensively over months to understand where every worker was, what their job was, and what their relationships with other workers were. We encouraged direct actions in the plant. Petitions, followed by marches on the human resources department, became a successful tactic, focusing on one production line at a time, whenever they were ready, and on any issues they felt strongly about. The company got the message that the disruptions could grow but they were far from ready to quit.

During the first year I was running the campaign, we crippled production twice, led by the incredible courage of the Latino workers, mostly from Mexico, who made up the majority of the workforce. The first walkout was a worker-initiated one-day strike with a march of five thousand area workers on May 1, 2006, that was part of the national "Day without a Latino" mobilization. The second was a protest that lasted two days in November 2006 after the company began illegally firing Latino workers for not providing valid social security numbers. These were powerful actions and extremely disruptive but still largely spontaneous, not part of a strategic plan and not easily repeated.

Following the November walkout, Smithfield started coordinating with ICE to deport undocumented workers, shifting the workforce to majority African American over the next six to nine months as Latino workers and leaders left, fearing more ICE raids.

On Martin Luther King Day that January, an African American–led petition for a paid holiday led to another serious disruption of production.

Still unanswered were the questions of how to strategically disrupt the most important link of the plant's operation, how much workers were willing to do, and how to take advantage of the growing "associative power" of our public campaign.

The kill floor was an obvious choke point, but it was a very large and sprawling department, and our support was not deep enough to act decisively. Yet a new opportunity began to evolve after the walkouts and other actions when, following a decade of NLRB litigation, Smithfield agreed to back pay for fired workers from the campaigns in the 1990s and one of those workers, a white male, was allowed to come back to work. He walked into the livestock department seeking to finish the organizing job he started in the 1990s. He quickly began building relationships in livestock, modeling pro-union behavior for the ninety-member department, largely African American with some Lumbi Native Americans. And he and others began working closely with our organizers.

Livestock met the bill for maximum impact. If the pigs can't get through livestock onto the kill floor, the rest of the plant has virtually nothing to do. Central to the Tar Heel plant's profitability was its vertical integration. Whereas most hog companies bought their hogs from independent hog raising companies, this NC plant grew its own through corporate-dominated contracts with small hog farmers surrounding the plant who raised eight million hogs a year for slaughter.

In the months following the Martin Luther King action we began working to assess and sign up every worker in the livestock department from the inside while we simultaneously visited them at home, often with a livestock leader and an organizer, to hear what their main issues were. Small actions began in the department with groups of workers challenging the supervisors, donning their yellow Justice@Smithfield T-shirts, writing "Union Time" on their hardhats and complaining to HR about problems.

To our astonishment, the issue workers brought up repeatedly was the lack of clean water to drink and soap and warm water to wash their hands. When you are forced to wallow in massive amounts of manure and pig sweat, and there is not a decent place to drink water or wash up before lunch, you get the message that the company doesn't care about you.

Once the outreach was done and our strength inside was tested, the workers began focusing their collective complaints on the lack of basic sanitary facilities. The company ignored them, while the temperatures rose daily in the southern May sun. As tension built, the workers finally decided to stop work one morning, just as the trucks were lining up and unloading. They simply sat down—all of them. They ignored the supervisor's threats and asked for the plant manager. The plant manager showed up and ordered them back to work, and they ignored him. The company came back with a letter threatening the workers, but they ignored it.

Meanwhile, the external organizers facilitated a call from livestock to OSHA who immediately called the plant manager. From our office we put the word out to our supporters around the country who started calling and emailing the company in large numbers, outraged at the mistreatment. The media were alerted and didn't believe us, but we were able to connect them to the workers sitting down in the plant, while management had no comment.

Most importantly, this was a choke point. The trucks were lining up and thousands of pigs were either squealing frantically in the trucks or stuck inside the gates heading toward the plant, with no workers to tend them. Once hogs get out of a truck, it's difficult to get them back in. Besides, there were thirty-two thousand hogs being primed for next day delivery on the assumption that these hogs would be slaughtered. With most of the other workers idle, this can get expensive quickly. But it only took ninety out of nearly five thousand workers to make it happen.

The company caved, well into the day, and promised immediate improvements. OSHA was now about to descend on the plant, the news media were onto the story and our allies and supporters all over the country were inspired by the workers' reports about the action. Eventually work resumed, but the workers made it clear that they would stop again if the problem wasn't fixed immediately. The company was cornered.

Word rocketed through the plant. No one was fired. Within days the company had a crew in the livestock area building a completely new break room area and running clean water into the department. The OSHA investigation kept the pressure on. The workers all over the plant were inspired, and more actions began being planned. In the following weeks the livestock workers led meetings during lunchtime in the front of the massive company cafeteria.

Although workers were unwilling to stop production long enough to bring the company to the table to negotiate with the union, this action marked a turning point. Within a couple of months the company started communicating with the national union leadership for the first time. Talks broke down by the fall, so the company filed what they called their "nuclear option," since all else was failing—a massive RICO lawsuit claiming that we were extorting them into accepting the union.

It would take another year for the company to realize that the lawsuit was not going to stop the campaign. Inside the plant, the day-to-day work of production was being constantly threatened by further walkouts on the kill floor and more challenges from the livestock workers, as seas of yellow T-shirts and helmets bearing the slogan "Union Time" signaled a national consumer and media campaign. With the RICO case hours away from going before the judge a deal was made in October 2008 that gave the union access to the inside of the plant and a fully empowered, round-the-clock, mutually selected monitor on site to keep the company in check during the six-week runup to an NLRB election. The union won the election. Within six months they signed a union contract with raises, safety and line-speed clauses, a good grievance procedure, and, most important, respect and dignity. The company decided they wanted to get back to the business of making money.

Chalk one up for choke points.

[The film about the Justice@Smithfield Campaign, *Union Time: Fighting for Workers Rights*, can be found at https://www.uniontimefilm. org.—Ed.]

Reflections on Ten Comradely Responses to the "Foundry Interviews"

John Womack Jr.

First, my gratitude for all the rich organizing experience refined into all the intelligence, insight, and wisdom in these comradely responses. It is harder (as Capt. James Gormley wrote) to be a comrade than a friend, different from being a brother or a sister. Comrades don't go easy on one another. They can't. They know the stakes are too high. They take you at your word. They don't quit on you. They make you do better. They keep you sharp. I am grateful for the comradely encouragement, questions, and criticism.

Second, I need to explain better why I have focused on the hired working class's industrial and technical power—and why I think this kind of power is strictly speaking the radical, critical power in modern capitalism. Here is a try: Human work is the source of all humanly produced value. In capitalism the value hired workers produce working the means of production that capitalists control all goes to the capitalists, who pay this class of workers enough to reproduce its capacity for orderly work tomorrow and as calculably needed in the future—and they keep all the rest, the surplus over orderly production and reproduction. This surplus value the capitalists dispose according to their class's interest, hugely over the last forty-odd years through finance, in part for their businesses old and new, but increasingly until definitively now not in production, but in financial speculation, the purer and simpler the better. They speculate on surplus value in gigantic swindles, which both plunder working-class savings and lay claim on future working-class income through lifelong working-class debt, briskly exchanged for profit in their financial markets. This is the new twist to capitalism, its new layer, more profitable than production to ever fewer, ever bigger capitalists. Systemically now capitalists pump all the surplus value they can, not into the extraction of new surplus value but into a great, cold financial brain insatiably quivering for the emptiest debt to sell as high and fast as it can, gambling the hired working class's surplus value in markets ideally of infinite risk.

Nevertheless, the critical point: Without work producing value, there is no surplus value. Capitalist capital lives on the hired working class's surplus value. Cut work for it, cut production for it, local up to systemic, and you cut off that much of the value it needs, its lifeblood, its oxygen. And if the cut is systemic, for long, you put that cold, calculating brain into shock.

I know you know this system of exploitation probably better than I do. And you get my strategic point, whether you agree with it or not. Capital will not surrender any of the surplus value it takes, for profits from investment or gambling, unless the hired working class forces the surrender however it can.

But I need to explain better too why I insist only on industrially and technically strategic power. I can give two reasons. One is only circumstantial. The other is analytical, as logical as I can make it, why from the very nature of the working class in capitalism I think this kind of power, industrial and technical, power over production, the power to produce or strike production, is the working class's specific, essential, radical, critical power.

As for the circumstantial, why so mulish about that one point? It befell me to work as an academic historian, 1965–2009. Academic labor history in the 1970s veered from the older generation doing "institutions," unions, to the younger generation excited about "the power of the people," mass action, every protest, every strike, every local rural rebellion, the start, it seemed, of the inevitable, natural, epic revolutionary struggle of all the oppressed to overthrow oppressive authority. Its patron saint was E.P. Thompson (whose "English working class," I recall, was preindustrial, and did not take into account Irish workers). Since then to date, with remarkable exceptions (which I emphasized in the book I can't get published in English), this has been the dominant, most popular theme in US, Canadian, and Mexican labor history. I thought too then it was a beautiful, inspiring theme, and how I wanted to write my Mexican labor history, "social history." But in 1973, doing research in Mexico City on the great general strikes there in 1916, I saw the Electrical Workers Union deliberately using its industrial power to make the strikes severely dangerous to capital's favorite Mexican revolutionaries then. The strikes involved masses of working people, mostly without organization, the city's wretchedly poor and starving, but importantly also unions of sweatshop, retail, and restaurant workers. But without the electrical workers' industrially strategic action to cut the city's power, these masses would have fast fallen into food riots, which capital's revolutionary army would have crushed. The strike led by electrical workers failed too; the army caught the strike committee in its hideout and court-martialed it. But the industrial force of the strike moved capital's revolutionary politicians to include recognition of the right to unionize and strike in Mexico's new constitution, 1917.

I could not get this kind of power out of my mind, and when I later studied the great Mexican railroad strikes of the 1920s I found it again in the Mexican Machinists Union. I wanted to explain it. I rediscovered Dunlop and wondered who besides him had seen the kind of power that he saw and, thanks to him, I thought I could understand. I went back to read in all the languages I could read through all the social science and history of labor since 1850, many business and labor publications too, right up into the 2000s, to find other conceptions, academic or in actual class struggles, of this kind of power. It was fascinating reading, for I found plenty to confirm my argument. But as I developed the argument, my fellow labor historians would not hear of it. I decided on a polemic against their social labor history, deliberately to provoke a debate with them, to clarify the differences between my argument and their assumptions. The polemic fizzled in an indignant muddle on the other side. Anyway, the argument in all the substance I could give it then went into the book published in Mexico in 2007, with 238 pages of footnotes and bibliography for whoever wants to go deeper.

Conceived as a polemic, the argument here still has a polemical edge and is provocative. This is especially why I am grateful to you comrades, Peter, Glenn, the ten others here, for taking it seriously, questioning it, making a comradely, dialectical debate where I hope we all in more light and perspective see all the points that matter to our common concern to end the exploitation and oppression of working people.

The logical reason for pulling toward that special strategic point: Strictly, specifically, the power of the hired working class as such is its power at its work, the power to work or not to work, not only in particular places, companies, and industries but also in the necessary connection, across places, companies, and industries, the power to connect or disconnect different technologies and industries, to deliver surplus value or stop delivery. This specifically working-class power concentrates at the material connections in production, between one technologically defined place to another in a company, likewise between technologically different companies in an industry, likewise between technologically different industries in an economy, national or global. Economists used to call it the "division of labor," not gendered or racial divisions but different productive divisions. Now it's the "supply chain." But it is therefore also the cooperation of labor, the connection of labor's divisions in production, the supply/demand chain. Whether you like it or not, this structure, this concentration, the positions at these connections, together are materially the case. This is strictly speaking, specifically, solely the working class's power in capitalism, the only power it alone as such has, technical and industrial, material power.

I need to make clear here, explicitly in the word "technological," the meaning I had obscured in the word "technical." I did not mean "technical," which I took from Dunlop in a sense he did not mean, that is, the new (post-Dunlop) sense of "tech," "high tech," the technology of electronics. This would make my argument useless except for "high tech"—absolutely not my intention. I meant "technical" in Dunlop's sense, the old, broad sense of tools, different kinds of them for different work, multiple technologies, different kinds of physical science, different kinds of engineering, mechanical, chemical, civil, electrical, nuclear, now electronic, etc., practically applied in particular detail and connected in particular combinations for the production of similar or different goods and services. Any workplace, company, industry, is a combination of technologies. Consider how many different technologies it takes in combination to produce coal or steel or oil, transport it, build bridges or cars, run airports, power plants, megaretail, a packing plant, a hospital, a university, an office park, even one office. Consider how many it takes just to make "high tech" or biotech go, including the technologies for HVAC. Technical power as I mean it is the power to use the technological connections between different operations and different departments in any working complex, use them for production, or break the connections and stop production. Industrial power as I mean it is the power to use or break the connections between different industries, effective on the economy at large. Both powers are material power, technical having microeconomic effects, industrial having macro effects.

But back to the logic of my mulishness on this point: In any working complex and between complexes, between industries, in the material supply/demand chain, the connections are many. And as connections, joints or links, couplings, connectors, interfaces, hinges, seams, or valves, things made to go precisely between things made, they need due maintenance or periodic replacement to keep them properly tight and the load on them right, for them to function properly for production (which includes transportation). Without maintenance, they will all on their own wear out, burn out, or break. Then they are bottlenecks, choke points, too much incoming, nothing outgoing, no intermediate or final product. But if the workers at the connection break it, not physically, but open or close it, prevent the transmission of products (including information), they too force a jam and a void, shutdown.

Here is the technically, industrially strategic key, not skills but positions: The material connections vary in importance by how much work depends on them, work on the incoming side and work on the outgoing side, how much interruption on both sides a break in the connection makes, how much work it stops, and how quickly. The more work a break stops, the faster the work stops, the more strategic that position is. Whoever can break the connection that can stop the most work the fastest, however they do it, whether they have technical skills, has technically the most strategic power, and if this stoppage spreads into an industry, it is industrially strategic power. It took no technical skill to flip a mill's main drive belt off weave-room line shafts, forcefully keep it off, to stop at once not only all the looms, but also quickly the precedent spinning, carding, drawing, slubbing, winding, warping, sizing, and looming work, and soon as well the finishing work. It took no technical skill to capture the dies at Fisher Body No. 1 and forcefully guard them, critical ground gained in the great GM strike, 1936–37. It is not the skill, but the position you take, hold, and use that matters. If you have comrades at work with you, you do not need techies to know who could take and hold the Walmart Mira Loma docks, take and hold the LA–Long Beach cranes, for working-class control of these hugely strategic links in US capital's productive supply/demand chain.

This is why I concentrate not on "the workplace," or "the point of production," or "sites of struggle," but on connected points, networks, complexes of struggle, connections, networks, and complexes that capital itself organizes and where it hires people to work. If you focus only on particular sites, you see often heroic struggles there, but on their own they typically in time weaken and fall apart, turn from epic to tragic. After sixty-five years studying them, the last fifty-five years professionally, I cannot see any natural power in them to stay strong for long where they are or to spread to other sites. They make history, but as local memorials, not as operational bases from which the struggle advanced to connect with other

bases, for new fronts in the struggle. It takes organization—conscious, deliberate, enduring connections with
other sites, none of which comes naturally, for coordinated,
purposeful growth into class struggle.

The question, then, is how you organize from a site to
sites to a combination of sites to class struggle. By struggle
I mean you fight to win, however long it takes, win for good.
The most famous successful examples are the Russian and
Chinese revolutions. What are the lessons they leave us
on this question, if any?

Both revolutions came from working people, in Russia
and China then by far mostly peasants, already in civil
struggles on their own against exploitation and oppression.
It may look like "peasants" means never applicable to the
USA. But if you think of "peasants" not by where they work,
out in the country, but how they produce value and lose
it, as workers at their own or rented means of production,
or only borrowed means to use, losing not on wages, but
in trade, it is not too stretchy to compare them with the
US self-employed, gigsters, contingents, and all the others
who are maybe hired but paid like indebted peons. Two
working classes, the hired and the daily trade-driven, or
two kinds of working class? Call them all together "working
people." On this account we would now have maybe forty
million "peasants," a quarter of US working people.

The comparison much harder to figure is between the
prerevolutionary civil struggles in Russia and China and
US civil struggles now. By the time the revolutionaries
moved to take power, in Russia in 1917, in China in 1945,
these struggles were already on a tremendous scale, in
their extent, force, and violence incomparable with civil
struggles ever (yet) known in the USA. Global wars, World
War I in Russia, wrecking the Czarist Empire, and World
War II in China, wrecking its bourgeois republic, had made
the struggles there multitudinous, tumultuous, terrific,

masses of people on their own overthrowing private and public powers for their own justice. But it is significant that they were typically in particular sites, multitudes of them, inspiring each other, yet each intent on its own struggle, for particular factories, particular land. They were multi-tudinous local revolts. Anxious Bolsheviks in 1917 asked Lenin about the party's program for peasants, land reform. He told them, as I remember reading, Don't worry about that now because all those soldiers, country boys quitting the war, deserting, coming home, they and their fathers are taking the land themselves. In China in 1926–27 Mao turned to the thousands of local peasant revolts in the interior provinces then. Even so, though these particu-laristic Russian and Chinese popular insurgencies were incomparably mightier than US sites in struggle ever have been, a look at how revolutionaries there organized them into massive revolutionary socialist movements may be instructive for organizing popular struggles here now at least into a powerful working people's movement.

Where did Lenin start organizing his revolution in 1917? Among thousands of popular struggles in Russia, then, Lenin concentrated on none involving peasants, whom (for the time being) he left basically to DIY, but on two industrial struggles, the two most strategic in Russia then, both hard to win because of conflicts with reformists: (1) in Petrograd, to control the port, the shipyards, and the arsenals; (2) on the railroads, for communication and trans-portation into the interior, to supply coal for the trains and food for the cities and to move the Red Army against coun-terrevolutionary armies. Both struggles the Bolsheviks won. Without these bases they could not have gained extensive popular support and made their revolution.

Where did Mao start organizing his revolution in 1927? Among thousands of peasant revolts in China then, his own party wrecked, he had no choice but a hard place, not where most revolts were, but in the mountains where he organized a small revolutionary armed force. As it gradually took over neighboring revolts, it organized, disciplined, and armed them, connected them with revolutionary forces in other provinces, and by redistributing land where it could to poor peasants gained strong support from them, made a Chinese Red Army. Fighting as it had to, as guerrillas, and taking no strategic positions, it hardly survived ten years of civil war with Western capital's Nationalist army. Only thanks to Japan's invasion of China in 1937 and in subordinate alliance with the Nationalist army, could Mao bring his army onto broad offensives. Still it could fight only a protracted war of maneuver, of which, however, it made the best: take no big strategic positions to hold, exhaust the enemy in his positions meanwhile by serving the poor, organize them for support, until your armed forces encircle the enemy and can overwhelm him. He falls apart and retreats, and your civil forces take the territory he abandons. So the Red Army had gained much ground and vast popular support in north China by 1945, though still no major strategic positions. Only when it received from the Soviet army in Manchuria immense bounties of surrendered Japanese weaponry did it begin regular campaigns to take and hold industrially strategic positions—especially strategic rail towns, coal districts, ports, then major industrial cities—until, as the People's Liberation Army, it smashed capital's Nationalist army and, with immense support from China's working people, took revolutionary command of all China's mainland in 1949.

The situation in the USA is now, to put it mildly, not propitious for these kinds of struggle. For all their distance from us, however, I think we can still draw from them many lessons about strategy in principle, since after all the principles are not new: Figure in cold blood what the present circumstances of power around you are, what you

want, how much you can win, how much you can risk, how
you can use the circumstances to your advantage, like an
ancient Greek general, where the best field is, when the best
time for your forces to fight to win. And fight not only tacti-
cally but operationally for your objectives. Nevertheless,
from the Russian and Chinese examples, from other specifically working people's struggles too, great and small, I
would draw another, modern lesson: In capitalism, working
people cannot win for good anything valuable if they do
not break for good capital's access to it, which means using
technical and industrial power in production to take and
hold it for working people, for their good.

The dialectic deserves a whole book, many books. But
let me try in a paragraph to explain how I understand it.
Any dialectic has to start on a particular point we can take
to be true while knowing it is only part of the truth. I start
on the modern working class as the class capital hires for
its profit to work on its means of production. The working
class is the class it is fundamentally and precisely because
it does this work. But this is not all it does, the fundamental
part, but only a part of all that makes it the working class.
Workers not only work, live on capital's wages in capital's
technological and industrial relations with one another.
They live also, in other contexts, not as "identities" but in
other human relations, emotional relations, in all the ways
they can and will. These relations, in the USA especially,
racial, ethnic, and gendered relations, are their daily life,
the daily living school in which they learn prejudice (and
may learn to grow out of it), learn greed, friendship, and
trust, despair and hope, in themselves and in others, and
may together learn class. This living school is the only
school in which they can learn class. From the elementary
truth of their work the dialectic is therefore now moving,
its course turning in social, political, legal, religious conditions into "association." This is a derivative, as I understand

it not a dismissal but a development, as in chemistry or math, a new function, dependent on the elementary truth, logically subsequent, subordinate to it, but a new part of the truth, together with work a larger truth, much more complicated, much richer and truer. From all the relations in this new, expanded truth some may organize, as they see themselves as workers, in unions, parties, for their power. This is another derivative, a new development into a bigger truth. And in yet a new development some may organize and fight for their vision of working-class power. No prior truth loses its truth in the new turns. All roll into every new truth to make the bigger new truth. The working class as actually lived is not (as Dunlop never claimed, and I never meant to claim) a stark set of economic and material relations. It is a continuously shifting, complex of various kinds of relations, stewing in its economic, material, social, political, religious divisions, never united, never fixed, always concretely in formation. In the USA its most divisive torment is white racism against black, brown, and Asian. Everywhere the class suffers from the divisions male chauvinism breeds.

But there is another dialectic, that of the hired working class's half-siblings and stepsiblings, the daily trade-driven at work, US "peasants." Where does their dialectic start? How does it develop? To my mind this is among the hardest working-class questions to understand, because these workers work in daily erratic relations and are continually coming into the hired class, though now they are continually much more leaving it, as capital expels them from it to work for capital on their own account. I will not even try to open any light here on a question so thickly complicated. I remark only that I think it is among the hired working class's most important strategic questions (as Lenin and Mao saw it was regarding their peasants). How can the hired working class, anyway its class-conscious organizations, earn the support of these supposedly independent but really trade-dependent workers, for a working people's alliance? How can the screwed-on-wages make an alliance with the screwed-on-trade? Recall the biggest recent US mass demonstrations, the Women's March and the March for Science in 2017, the March for Our Lives in 2018, the Second Women's March in 2019. These masses were all largely if not overwhelmingly of working people. What if they had been proudly, publicly "Working People's Marches" for women's equality, for science in public policy, against guns in worker-on-worker violence? If only…

Many other significant questions I wish I could treat seriously here, but I am already way over my limit. Here are fifteen on which, in no order, I offer the briefest of comments.

Spartacus: Certainly he did right to fight to liberate slaves. Only from the little we know about him he did not intend to abolish slavery but rescue as many as he could, lead them north into Gaul, and let them go home. Good enough! And he was brilliant with tactics but was not much on strategy. He could have shut Rome the city down and disabled its available army if he had jammed a couple big Roman aqueducts and knocked holes in their sides, and then headed north, not south.

Operation Dixie: Stupid and racist at the time, never mind in retrospect. Textiles were big in the Carolinas, but nothing strategic Dixie-wide. Tobacco? Militant, heroic black workers, but no strategic power even in states where they were strongest. To bust Dixie why didn't the CIO go strong for Birmingham, Atlanta, Norfolk and Charleston, shipyards, Memphis, capital there all then fat on wartime federal contracts? Go for them to desegregate white racist unions and to win black civil rights as well?

Internationalism: Good question, nothing on it in the interviews. I start with capitalist imperialism, which is why working classes everywhere need internationalism. In old days, when capital's international money was gold, US capital pushed to make the USA the world's industrial superpower. It counted on borders for tariffs on competitive imports. This suited US white workers, who could hog the world's best-paying jobs. Ergo, US white working-class economic and political nationalism. Since about 1970, when US capital quit gold, converted international money to the US dollar, it has pushed "globalization," its own international freedom to invest dollars anywhere it can, making the USA the world's financial powerhouse, locating industrial production wherever in the world it is cheapest. Dollarized imperialism also counts on borders, but to control immigration as it needs labor, meanwhile keeping labor on one side of the border in competition with labor on the other side, for the most profit from both sides. It therefore abhors labor's internationalism. And this suits workers who have lost jobs but don't see capital's trick. Ergo, still, among white, black, and Latino workers, much economic and political nationalism.

How then in the USA now do you grow international solidarity? I doubt right now you can do any more than education. But don't expect much from moral education: "Love workers in other countries as yourselves." Get quickly into econ-political education, about US imperialism. Dollarized imperialism, capital's contempt for borders but imposition of them on labor, foments nationalism, the bane of the international working-class solidarity and chances for cooperation. But if for this education you organize programs, avoid all official agencies, federal, state, county, municipal, and all political parties. Try two other, parallel courses: (1) programs of live, direct international exchanges, small, but as many as you can, like sister cities, working people's sisterly exchanges, to learn mutual concern and solidarity; (2) programs in unions, which given the AFL-CIO's inveterate Cold-Warism would have to be in caucuses, to teach how dollarized imperialism rewards a few but screws workers everywhere, whereas working people's internationalism is both an obstacle to war and the grounds for joint industrial action for their mutual benefit. Strategically, technically, and industrially, just think of the logistics of international transportation and communications.

Social justice unionism: What good soul could oppose it, not fight hard for it? If you can get unions to do it, like the ILGWU in Los Angeles, more power to you and your union. Only remember, you are assuming capitalism, which means whatever justice you win you are liable soon to lose.

Workers making ripples? See how they spread! But see too how as they spread they weaken, and then die down. How do workers make tidal waves, tsunamis, against capitalism?

Association, a second take, in practice: I already argued why I think it's a consequence of the elementary truth in capitalism, as I see it, that capital hires people for its profit to work its means of production for a wage that is only part of the value these people collectively produce. If there were no such category of people, there would be no workers to associate. But how do they associate, specifically as workers? What gets them to do it? What moves them in this association into working-class action? Is it "spontaneous," as both Engels and Luxemburg believed? Lenin thought not. Nor did E.O. Wright. I don't either. "Spontaneity" might give you self-defense, resistance, struggle within capitalism for reforms of law or the paid contract for your shop, your union, your industry. It will not give you struggle against capitalism for your class. I respect Wright on "association," especially for his critiques of others on the concept. I follow him on "associational power." But if it is not "spontaneous," how do you make it

happen, and how then do you make it most effective? Trial
and error? Strategically? What determines the strategy?
Wright gives no practical advice. I think Perrone had it
right. You have to wound capital to make it yield anything.
And you wound it painfully, grabbing its attention, when
you take direct material action to stop its production, cut
its profit.

Beverly Silver: Her *Forces of Labor* (2003), coming out
of "world-systems" sociology, is good on associational practice. It's in one of the last three bits I want to finish for
that manuscript I hope to publish in English. She relied
especially there on a younger contemporary of Dunlop's,
Benson Soffer, who had served on the Wage Stabilization
Board. He had focused on skilled workers' power in their
labor markets, in association in their own interest, not
to force employers technically, much less industrially, to
cough up for the broader working-class good.

"Internal organizing… *reorganizing*": Yes! These sepa-
rately entrenched regiments of organized labor make it
hard for a labor movement to move. I see them as business unionism in full array. This kind of unionism has
from the beginning stood strong in US labor, strongest in
the AFL and railroad brotherhoods. The Wagner Act legit-
imized industrial unions, some fighting then for broad
working-class objectives. But it also established that the
most any union under its protection could fight to win was
a collective contract for its members. Quasi-corporatist,
unlike national labor law in Canada or postwar Western
Europe, the Wagner Act practically ordered that the US
labor movement develop as specifically interested groups,
no status class-wise, class-wide. And since then, a few
remarkable exceptions aside, US unions have looked first
and mainly for US legal protection from above, the NLRB,
not for extralegal solidarity from other US unions, class-
wise. For their own contractual interests, however much

the AFL-CIO may urge support for an affiliate's struggle, the rule is still each bunch on its own contract. In this array the filthiest sin is the raid, the theft of a contract, membership, dues.

In the USA a working-class strike, say to secure a fund to which workers for eighty-five years have contributed, Social Security, is legally out of the question. In the USA "class action" is a bourgeois, civil affair, in another dimension from working-class action. Railroad labor law is even more difficult for working-class action. The greatest move forward I can now imagine for US labor would be to combine the ILWU, the ILA, the IBT, the IAM, and the UTU into a US Transport and General Workers' Union. This is not a matter of numbers, elections; it is a matter of nationally strategic industrial power. I cannot imagine the executive officers of any of these unions hearing such a thought, because they know what it would mean. Nor can I imagine most of the membership of these unions seeing why they should risk what they now have for what a USTGWU could do. How then even to start on it? Internal organizing, "association," yes, your caucuses, but in serious, strategically minded connection with caucuses in other unions, joint internal organizing, which might well take a decade or a generation to consolidate, and then in yet another capitalist crisis take extralegal action to force the issue and win.

Labor's solidarity with "minorities," who are, say, 90 percent working-class—this is not only social justice. It is obviously also in labor's interest. The obstacles are also obvious, tough, endemic, abiding: capital and its politicians, of course, but add as well working-class white racism, male chauvinism, contractualism. Moreover, "minorities" as a statistic is only a suggestion of organizing possibilities, no guide to organizing action. And these minorities, as connected communities of workers, are difficult to organize

when the work they do is almost always nothing industrially strategic. How does labor beat the obstacles if the
minorities work in a big city's garment sweatshops? Once
upon a time in New York City the ILGWU would organize
the cutters (Jewish men), have them strike, which would
stop all the other work (mostly Jewish and Italian women),
jam the New York business, make a huge commercial stink,
and win some good. In LA in the 1970s it was much more
complicated; technically, many cutting shops are separate from sewing shops; ethnically, many undocumented
Mexican women are in sewing and other semiskilled work,
with undocumented Mexican men and women at unskilled
work. The AFL-CIO, therefore the ILGWU too, nationally
opposed employment of undocumented workers, backed
tight, strict limits on immigration. But despite national
leadership, as the UFW turned to support the undocumented, the California ILGWU, in league with veteran
Mexican-American organizers, unionized them in the LA
garment business and soon transformed the LA County
Federation of Labor into a US powerhouse of working
people's international, racial, ethnic, and gender solidarity.
In this struggle you had spontaneity galore, heroic devo-
tion, massive "association."

But to organize it, encircle the enemy, overwhelm him,
three sociopolitically strategic keys: the California ILGWU's
recognition of its own interest, its long public collabora-
tion with other California unions in broad working-class
causes, and its deep, vital reliance on institutions and
organizations long embedded in LA's Mexican-American
communities.

Compare Chicago. Without labor's multiunion, force-
ful commitment, largely on heroic organization in black
and Latino communities, the struggle there took almost
another, murderous decade to elect Harold Washington
(1984), and when he died it all fell back on the communities.

Not until the Chicago Teachers Union, despite the Chicago Federation of Labor, turned strong to "social unionism" (2010) did an alliance of a big multipowered union and organized communities begin to lay the strategic ground to fight capital's Daley-ite management of the city.

Chiapas? The EZLN was at a far, distant cry, spectacular tactics, an ideology, a wing and a prayer for strategy. In the end no power, only dead heroes, saints, and poetry.

Harry Braverman: Decades ago I read that brilliant book. And there I saw Marx's point that technology mattered in class. Braverman's light still shines bright for me. His book should be on every organizer's list of required readings. Only I see two problems: (1) It is mostly about "deskilling," skilled workers defending their privileged positions, and their resistance, not (as I read it) about offense, them taking their positions to use for their class; (2) it leaves the gloomy impression workers lose all in a new technology of production (e.g., Fordism). In all due respect for Braverman, I argue not about skills but about positions, and I think any modern production is inevitably a combination of technologies, old and new, a combination of divisions of labor. Workers can break that combination, to their benefit.

How do you fight with IT? See where its material connections are. Check Steven Aftergood's Federation of American Scientists releases of Congressional Research reports on "critical infrastructure," or just search for "critical infrastructure" or "cyber warfare." The Pentagon and the military press will tell you. And then look into IT's logistics, its mundane needs, its bread and fodder and water—and latrines.

Are health-care and educational workers "material"? I know from my sisters and my children the blessed quality of soul these workers may have. And I have to clarify I distinguish between "economic," all the relations in production and finance, and "material," the physical relations at the means of production. Let me take the question here to mean whether these workers have positions in the technology of their work or industrial positions in the economy so that in battles with capital they can make it knuckle under. Yes, if not only "associated" but actually sticking together, moving together at the right time materially against their employer, they may well get good results. How much does this matter economically? In seventeen states the biggest employer is a health-care system. Altogether health-care workers may be 15 percent of the US labor force. In seven states the biggest employer is the state university system. But look nationally how many kindergarten, primary, and secondary public school-teachers there are, maybe 8 percent of the labor force. This is nationally massive economic power. If these workers move small, they may win small. If they move big, they may win really big, economically, against capital, for themselves and their class. But how would it be material? First, directly, when it stops work for capital and resumes work for the working class. Second, indirectly, because health care and education are the precondition of production, the restoration and reproduction of working people's physical, mental, and moral powers to produce, in capitalism for capital, or otherwise for their people now and to come.

The political elite: In capitalism, why concentrate on it when what determines what it does is capital? If you dump one part of the elite for another, but capital runs it too, what good does it do?

"Essential workers": These responses all arrived before the new plague, and before we could read in the bourgeois press how in public-health crises people depend not only on health-care workers and school workers, but also on firefighters, meatpacking, farm and cannery workers, USPS workers, public-transport workers, supermarket workers, janitors, garbage collectors, rail workers, truck drivers, car

mechanics, gas and electrical workers, police, and tele-
communication workers. Wait until the wildfire season in
the West begins, hurricane season in the South and East,
and see how many more essential workers there are. In
"essential" I see "technically essential," urgently necessary
to the daily reproduction of our capacity to work as well as
to the continuing production (including delivery) of vital
supplies, not only now but always. Taken for granted, most
workers are not unionized, not militantly defended, and
wretchedly paid. If this plague lifts soon, will capital's
labor market (its "wage structure") naturally change to fork
over more to them for their essential work? Will the feds?
(Check who owns the senators and reps who vote against
FEMA's budgets.) On the invisible or the visible hand I bet
my Social Security check not. If the plague does not lift,
or soon returns, or when the next plague descends, will
these workers spontaneously associate in revolt if only to
protect themselves, take housing, food, and supplies that
no government provides but that they need for the essential work they do? Likewise, with a few remarkable, heroic
exceptions, I bet not. It would take organization, organized
connections, strategic connections of all kinds, to secure
working people's health and safety then.

The School! In old days, a century ago, working people
had many labor colleges all around the USA, often union-
funded schools, within AFL locals, but against business
unionism, for "social unionism." States and cities also
offered higher education specifically for working people
who were high school grads, agricultural and mechanical
colleges, Wayne State, CCNY, though primarily to educate
them for trades, business, or professional careers, not to
fight for their class. It's very different now, but is it impossible to start new labor colleges, for students of all ages,
for education on class? Is it pie in the sky to propose a
US working people's institute of technology for research

and teaching on strategic connections of all kinds, especially capital's technical and industrial vulnerabilities?
This could be the school to train the US working people's
general staff and cadres for class struggle. This is related
to another required reading, which is beautifully practical:
Palmiro Togliatti, *Lectures on Fascism* [given in Moscow in
1935 to Italian refugees from fascism]. Along similar lines,
then, why not an international working-class institute for
strategic studies?

Epilogue? No, an Update and Directions

━━━━

These interviews of four years ago and the responses since then of our comrades call for more than an epilogue. For our little book to do what we hope it does, show workers how they can work their power at work for their collective interest, it warrants at least a summary update after the last two weird years—and maybe as well some words on the struggles ahead.

The biggest, weirdest, most disruptive turn has been the COVID plague. All over the world it has hit working people hardest, killing millions of them, throwing hundreds of millions out of work, and making other work heavier, more dangerous. And it has messed with minds, because at work, off work, at meetings, at home, or out for a break from their worries, working people are mostly used to company, and they read faces more easily than public advisories or mandates. For them, especially, "social distancing" and masks have often been unnatural. The plague has caused mischief with their unions too, if they have them, public health now imposing duties not in a union's contract. Worse, if for no more reason than global changes in climate, more plagues are coming. What if the world is going to be all different now, is all we have learned useless?

No, breathe deep and refocus. Through all this hard, divisive complication, millions of workers in the USA at least have also enjoyed The Great Resignation, i.e., they have taken the initiative and got better new jobs. So many have quit old jobs for safer and higher-paying jobs that nationwide (nominal) hourly wages have been averaging ever higher. And some strikers have won new benefits and raises to cut their losses to inflation.

But you organizers, refocus strategically: Most important for the labor movement, many jobs in manufacturing, transportation (land, water, and air), warehousing, and construction, are increasing faster than the average increase in overall employment, or at least as fast as average, and on the most credible projections they will be increasing fast for a decade or more. For labor these are strategic industries, and the jobs on fast increase, hundreds of thousands of them, are at technically strategic positions. Check the Bureau of Labor Statistics, *Occupational Outlook Handbook* online, A–Z Index, for example, "Industrial Machinery Mechanics, Machinery Maintenance Workers, and Millwrights," or "Passenger Vehicle Drivers," or "Hand Laborers, Freight, Stock, and Material Movers."[1] The increase projected for industrially and technically strategic positions is far from the huge increase projected for jobs such as home health and personal care aide. But from a strategic perspective it is incomparably more important. In economically strategic industries workers at technically strategic jobs will have extraordinary collective power over US production, profit, and capital, and so will have new power in national politics. If deliberately organized, they could use the power for all working people's sake.

Besides COVID, the biggest economic agitation has been over kinks in the world's supply chains—choke points, or bottlenecks, where our technically strategic positions are. From the hullaballoo about these choke points, one might think it was COVID that caused them all. No, they were there long before COVID. It made them worse, but it did not cause them. And when COVID subsides, if another bug does not quickly make a new plague, choke points will no longer choke so much business. But bottlenecks will still be there, slowing supplies of necessary parts and highly demanded products.

These mismatches of supply and demand are inevitable for every economy but Robinson Crusoe's. If you have any trade between any more complicated economies, even between firms, or any technical division of labor in production, simultaneous or sequential dependence in the phases of production, you run into bottlenecks at the connections, the seams, articulations, links, junctions, bonds, intersections, forks, and bifurcations. Nothing human can ever be free of them, perfectly efficient—most certainly, most obviously, not trade or production. Businesses have long known that well. They pay for studies to find their bottlenecks and eliminate them, which only leads to new bottlenecks. A brilliant British socialist economics professor nearly eighty-five years ago published his explanation of how firms deal with them. He never mentioned choke points or bottlenecks, or anything "strategic." But his argument about "costs" clarified the economically universal inevitability of inherent problematic connections in trade and production, and thereby revealed the strategic value in the connections of the workers there. Its significance still decades later (not then fully understood) won him a Nobel Prize in "Economic Sciences."[2]

In short, think: As long as there is more than Robinson Crusoe, much work will critically, strategically, depend on some other work. If businesses seek to control it, then you, organizers, organize to control it—for labor's sake, for working people's sake.

Acknowledgments

John Womack Jr. thanks all from whom he learned all he knows about work, working people, organizing, justice, and social movements. He thanks especially James Brennan, Oliver Dinius, and Miles Rodríguez, who in their doctoral studies taught him much about workers' technical and industrial action in Argentina, Brazil, and Mexico, and Ingrid Bleynat, whose doctoral studies taught him much about some workers who were not "on-hire": the small-scale vendors in the municipal markets of nineteenth- and twentieth-century Mexico City. He owes special thanks too to Alicia Hernández Chávez, who managed publication in Mexico of *Posición estratégica y fuerza obrera*, and to Peter Olney and Glenn Perušek, who conceived this project, organized it, carried it all along, and here brought it to completion. Olney thanks his co-collaborator Glenn Perušek and his favorite uncle, John S. Bowman, for his helpful editorial and content suggestions.

Selected Historical Biographies

Eugene Victor Debs (1855–1926) was born in Terre Haute, Indiana, quit school at fourteen, worked as a greaser, painter, and car cleaner in the Vandalia Railroad Terre Haute shops; and as a locomotive fireman, Vandalia RR (1871–75). He joined the Brotherhood of Locomotive Firemen (1875), served as grand secretary of BLF (1880–93) and editor of BLF monthly *Firemen's Magazine* (1880–94). Debs led the organization of the American Railway Union (1893), among the largest and first industrial unions in United States, and was its president (1893–97). He led the ARU's Great Northern Railway Strike (1893) and led the ARU into the 1894 Pullman Strike ("Debs's Rebellion"), which was broken by the US Army and for which Debs spent six months in jail (1895), where he read Marx's *Capital* and Kautsky on German social democracy. Debs left jail a socialist. He was the Socialist Party of America presidential candidate from 1900 to 1920, garnering more than nine hundred thousand votes in 1912. Urging US neutrality in World War I, he was sentenced to ten years in federal prison for an antiwar speech delivered in Canton, Ohio, in 1918. His sentence was commuted in 1921, but prison had broken his health. Debs died in 1926 in Elmhurst, Illinois; he was buried in Terre Haute.

Farrell Dobbs was born in Queen City, Missouri (1907), the son of a coal yard worker. Growing up in Minneapolis, he graduated from Minneapolis North High School (1925) and worked his way up from wireman to planning engineer at Western Electric (1925–31). He quit to enter small business to pay for law school, failed, and although unemployed, remained pro-Hoover in 1932. Dobbs worked in Pittsburgh Coal's Minneapolis yards (1933–34) and joined General Truck Drivers and Helpers Local 574 of the AFL-affiliated International Brotherhood of Teamsters (IBT; 1933). He was a militant organizer of strikes in Minneapolis (1933–34) and a picket dispatcher in the trucker strikes. He joined the (Trotskyist) Communist League of America (CLA), was elected to Local 574's negotiating committee (1934), appointed Local 574 staff director (1934–37), and elected Local 574 (rechartered as Local 544 in 1936) secretary-treasurer (1934–39). Dobbs organized the IBT's eleven-state North Central Council (1937), led its negotiating committee to a twelve-state master contract (1938), and mentored Jimmy Hoffa in organizing the IBT out of Detroit across the Midwest. Dobbs was elected the Socialist Workers' Party (SWP) national labor secretary (1940–46). Convicted of sedition under the Smith Act, he served thirteen months in the Sandstone, Minnesota, federal penitentiary (1944–45). He was editor of the SWP's *The Militant* (1943–48) and the SWP's candidate for mayor of New York (1945) and president (1948, 1952, 1956, 1960). Dobbs was SWP national chair (1949–53) and national secretary (1953–72). He wrote *Teamster Rebellion* (1972), *Teamster Power* (1973), *Teamster Politics* (1975), and *Teamster Bureaucracy* (1977), among other books and pamphlets. Farrell Dobbs died in Pinole, California, in 1983.

John Thomas Dunlop, born in Placerville, CA (1914), was schooled on Cebu, Philippines, where his parents were Presbyterian missionaries. His first major article, "The

Movement of Real and Money Wage Rates" (*Economic Journal* 48, no. 191 [September 1938]: 413–34) corrected Keynes on wages in slumps. Dunlop earned a PhD in economics, University of California–Berkeley (1939), with a dissertation titled "Movements of Wage-Rates in the Business Cycle." Starting in 1938, he held teaching and administrative positions at Harvard for the rest of his life. Physically exempt from conscription in World War II, Dunlop cofounded with Sumner Slichter and James J. Healy the Harvard Trade Union Program (1942). He was chief of the Research and Statistics Branch of the National War Labor Board (1943–45), directing Clark Kerr, Benjamin Aaron, and other later distinguished labor economists in detailed, urgent studies to pacify industrial class conflicts in US defense plants and strategic infrastructure. Dunlop's first book, *Wage Determination under Trade Unions* (1944) was "impressive and stimulating" in Maurice Dobb's professional judgment. Among other positions, Dunlop was a member of the National Relations Labor Board (1948–52) and was US secretary of labor (1973–75) before resigning over presidential veto of legislation to strengthen union picketing rights. His professional articles on labor and management, from 1938 to 1998, number more than one hundred. Among his other books, with Clark Kerr et al., *Industrialism and Industrial Man: The Problems of Labor and Management in Economic Growth* (1960); with Derek Bok, *Labor and the American Community* (1970). Dunlop died at the age of eighty-nine in Boston (2003).

The four **Dunne brothers**, William (Bill) Francis, Vincent Raymond, Grant John, and Miles Bernard, were the sons of an Irish immigrant father, who was a laborer in railroad construction and a logger. Their mother worked at home, raising nine children in Central Minnesota farm country. As boys, all four worked as farmhands.

Bill Dunne was born in Kansas City, Missouri (1887). He attended the College of St. Thomas in St. Paul, Minnesota; in penury he quit before graduating (1907). He worked as an electrician in Northern Pacific Railroad shops across Montana (1907–8) and as wireman for Independent Telephone, Rocky Mountain Bell, and Pacific Telephone and Telegraph in Montana, Idaho, and Washington (1908–12). He joined the AFL-affiliated International Brotherhood of Electrical Workers (IBEW) and the Socialist Party of America (SPA), agitating for workers convicted of bombing the *Los Angeles Times* (1910). In Spokane, he was a prizefighter (1912) and an electrician for the British Columbia Electric Railway in Vancouver (1912–16). Bill was elected business agent for IBEW Local 213 in Vancouver (1913), vice president of the British Columbia Federation of Labor, vice president of the Pacific District Council of Electrical Workers, and IBEW district organizer in British Columbia, Washington, Oregon, and Idaho (1914–16). Deported from Canada for opposing World War I (1916), he returned to Montana, working as an electrician for the Chicago-Milwaukee-St. Paul-Pacific Railroad and for Timber Butte Mining (1916–17). He was elected chair of the strike committee for IBEW Local 65 (Butte), which conducted a wartime strike against Montana Power (which served Butte mining companies, e.g., Anaconda). He allied Local 65 and the new (non-AFL) Metal Mine Workers Union in Butte, was elected Local 65 business agent, and led allied strikes for weeks before the Montana Federation of Labor broke them (1917). Bill gave the eulogy for Industrial Workers of the World (IWW) leader Frank Little, who was murdered in Butte. Bill was the cofounding editor of the socialist *Butte Bulletin* (1917), which berated capitalists, the AFL, and the United States at war; hailed the Russian Revolution; defended the IWW's wartime copper strike in Butte; and advocated for the release of Eugene V. Debs and the IWW members convicted of sedition (1918). Bill was convicted under the Montana state sedition law in 1919 (overturned). He was Nonpartisan League/Democratic candidate for state representative (1918) winning one term. In the legislature, he filed the first bill in the US for the withdrawal of US troops from Russia and for the recognition of Soviet Russia. A cofounding member of the Communist Labor Party in Chicago (1919), he thereby went into the Workers Party of America (WPA) in 1921. Bill was elected to the WPA's central executive committee and executive council (1922–26), appointed to the *Daily Worker* editorial committee (1923), expelled from the AFL (1923), appointed to the WPA's executive council's political committee (1924–26), and became editor of the *Daily Worker* in Chicago and New York City (1924–28). He was the WPA delegate to the fifth Comintern congress and candidate for its executive committee, was appointed to the executive committee of the Communist International's organization bureau (1924) and was elected to Workers (Communist) Party (W[C]P) central executive committee (1925), backing William Foster against the anti-Stalinist "City College boys" in W(C)P's strife (1925–28). He was the W(C)P's delegate to the Red International of Labor Unions (RILU) fourth congress and the sixth Comintern congress (1928), fiercely breaking with his brothers who followed the Trotskyists expelled from the WPA (1928). He served as a Comintern journalist in the Mongolian People's Republic (1928–29), was elected to the new Communist Party USA's (CPUSA) central committee and political committee (1929), and was elected to the national committee of the Trade Union Unity League (TUUL; 1929–35). He organized for the National Textile Workers Union; National Miners Union; Steel and Metal Workers Industrial Union; International Longshore and Warehouse Union; International Union of Mine, Mill and Smelter Workers; and American Newspaper

Guild (1929–38). Along the way, he was personnel director for US workers at the Stalingrad tractor factory (1931–32), was again editor of the *Daily Worker* (1934–36), served in the US merchant marine (1943–45), and was expelled from the CPUSA for "left sectarianism" (1946). Bill was author of numerous pamphlets including *Gastonia: Citadel of the Class Struggle in the New South* (1929), *The Great San Francisco General Strike* (1934), (with Morris Childs) *Permanent Counter-Revolution: The Role of the Trotzkyites in the Minneapolis Strikes* (1934); and *The Struggle against Opportunism in the Labor Movement* (1947). He cofounded the James Connolly Association in New York (1951). Bill died in New York City in 1953.

Vincent "Ray" Dunne was born in Kansas City, Kansas (1889). In 1903–4, he was a migrant worker from Minnesota to Montana. He joined the IWW in Montana (1904) and was an IWW "free-speech" agitator in Seattle and Los Angeles (1907). He worked in a Louisiana sawmill, on an Arkansas road gang, and in a Texas diner (1908). Back to Minnesota in 1909, he was an IWW teamster in Minneapolis (1910–14). He worked as laborer, hauler, weighmaster, dispatcher, and superintendent in Minneapolis coal yards (1914–33) and was a member of the General Truck Drivers and Helpers Local 574 (Minneapolis) of the International Brotherhood of Teamsters (1914–33). Ray joined the SPA in 1915, was a delegate to the AFL-affiliated Minneapolis Central Labor Union (1918–26), and joined the Communist Party of America (1920), the WPA (1921), and the Minneapolis Farmer-Labor Party (F-LP; 1921–28). Ray was expelled from the IBT (1926), was WPA candidate for US Senate in Minnesota, and was expelled from the WPA and the F-LP (1928). He was a member of the (Trotskyist) CLA (1928–34) and led their efforts inside Local 574 (1933–34). He also led strikes in Minneapolis (1934) and was a picket dispatcher in the trucker strikes (1934). Trotsky called him the "most effective labor leader in America." He cofounded the (Trotskyist) Workers Party of the United States (WPUS; 1934–36). He was editor of the Local 574-backed Northwest Labor Unity Conference's *Northwest Organizer* (1935–36). When the IBT revoked Local 574's charter in 1935, Ray was appointed to the committee that negotiated a new IBT charter in 1936 as Local 544. In 1936, Ray was the SPA's Minnesota state organizer and SPA candidate for mayor of Minneapolis. He was expelled from the SPA and joined the Socialist Workers' Party (SWP) in 1937. He led Local 544 into affiliation with the CIO but lost it back to the AFL-affiliated national IBT (1941). Convicted with Dobbs under the Smith Act (1941), he spent thirteen months in Sandstone penitentiary (1943–45). He was SWP candidate for mayor of Minneapolis (1943, 1947), SWP national labor secretary (1946–56), and SWP Minnesota candidate for US Senate (1952, 1954). He served as SWP chair in Minnesota (1959–64) and was SWP national organizer against the US war on Vietnam (1965–70). Ray died in Minneapolis in 1970.

Grant John Dunne, born near Little Falls, Minnesota (1894), was a migrant worker in Minnesota logging and railroad construction (1906–9). He attended high school for one year at Minneapolis South High School, then worked as a clerk for Railway Express and then for Crane Plumbing, in Minneapolis (1910–18). As a private in the Third Pioneer Infantry (engineers) of the US First Army, he saw action in the Meuse-Argonne offensive, and was hospitalized for shell shock (1918–19). He was a clerk, branch manager, and estimator for a plumbing-supply house in St. Louis (1920–30), a coal handler and hauler in Minneapolis (1931–34), and a member of the CLA (1931–34). He recruited Dobbs into Local 574 and was a member of the Local 574 organizing committee, strike committee, and negotiating committee, and served as recording secretary in Minneapolis during strikes (1934). A militant in the WPUS (1934–36) and SPA (1936–37), he was reelected Local 544 (successor local to 574) recording secretary (1936–39). Expelled from the SPA, he was a member of the SWP from 1937. Grant served as general organizer of Local 544 (1939–40). Indicted under the Smith Act, he committed suicide in Minneapolis (1941).

Miles "Mick" Dunne was born near Little Falls, Minnesota (1895), and graduated Minneapolis South High School (circa 1913). He was a telephone lineman in Minneapolis (circa 1913–18). Drafted into the US Army, he was a corporal in the Signal Corps in France (1918) and worked again as a lineman in Minneapolis (1918–29). He joined the CPA (1920) and the WPA (1921) but was expelled from the WPA (1928). He was a militant in the CLA (1928–34), worked as a coal handler and hauler in Minneapolis (1931–34), and joined Teamster Local 574 in 1931. A member of the CLA (1933–34), he was also secretary of Local 574 in 1934, and was a member of Local 574's organizing committee, strike committee, and negotiating committee in the Minneapolis strikes (1934), and a WPUS member (1934–36). He was assigned by Local 574 to lead IBT Local 173 in Fargo, North Dakota, to unionize the unorganized. He led strikes (which the national IBT broke) (1934–35). A member of the SPA (1936–37) and the editor of *Northwest Organizer* (1936–41), he became a member of the SWP (1937). He was elected Local 544 secretary treasurer (1938–40) and was editor of the *Industrial Organizer* (1941–42). He was indicted under the Smith Act and acquitted (1941). He was president of Local 544-CIO (a Trotskyist shell) (1941–45). Blacklisted after the war, he did odd jobs. Mick Dunne died in Minneapolis (1958).

William Edward Foster, aka William Z. Foster, was born in Taunton, Massachusetts (1881), the son of immigrants (his father was Irish, a stableman, and revolutionary Fenian, his mother was English, Catholic, and a textile worker who raised nine children). He grew up in Philadelphia, was baptized and catechized Roman Catholic. Quitting school at ten, he apprenticed in metal molding, and in 1895 he joined demonstrations for striking Philadelphia streetcar workers. He worked (1894–1907) from Pennsylvania to Florida to New York to Texas to Oregon in a type foundry, a white-lead factory, and a fertilizer plant; on railroad construction gangs; as a longshoreman and sailor; and along the way was a hobo, logger, swamper, and a streetcar motorman, among others. In 1901, he was co-organizer of Manhattan's Third Avenue motormen and conductors (an AFL affiliate). Foster joined the SPA in Portland (1901), the Wage Workers Party in Spokane, and the IWW (1909). Traveling to Europe, he studied the French and German labor movements (1910–11) and reported on the French National Railway Workers strike (1910). Returning to the United States, he founded the Syndicalist League of North America in Chicago (1912). He worked as a railroad brakeman and fireman (1911–12), and as a railroad interchange-car-inspector in Chicago yards, and he was a member of the AFL-affiliated Brotherhood of Railway Carmen (1912–17).

Foster was appointed AFL general organizer in Chicago (1915). He cofounded the (syndicalist) International Trade Union Educational League (1915), was elected business agent of the Chicago Railway Carmen (1916) and led the Chicago Federation of Labor (AFL-affiliated) to form the Stockyards Labor Council to federate old and new pack-inghouse unions, including black workers in federal locals, and thereby force unionism and collective contracts on Chicago meatpacking companies. Foster led the massive wartime Chicago packinghouse strike (settled by the AFL in government arbitration) in 1918. In 1918, Foster was elected secretary of the AFL's National Committee for Organizing

Iron and Steel Workers (fifteen AFL unions). He organized the national steel strike (1919–20), which affected all big mills from New York to Colorado, half of the national industry, before being broken by state and federal forces.

Foster was founder and secretary-treasurer of the Trade Union Educational League (TUEL; 1920–29). In Moscow, he gained the TUEL's affiliation with the Comintern's RILU (1920). He joined the Workers Party of America, was elected to its central executive committee and executive council (1921) and was subsequently reelected and appointed to the executive council's political committee and organization committee (1923–25). His prosecution under Michigan law for criminal syndicalism (1923) ended in a mistrial. He was WPA candidate for president (1924); WPA delegate to the fifth Comintern congress, elected to the Comintern's executive committee (1924), and elected WPA national chair (1924–25). Via the WPA he went into the Workers (Communist) Party (W[C]P); he was elected to its central executive committee, executive council, and political committee. As secretary of the W(C)P's industrial department (1925–29), he led the TUEL in founding the National Textile Workers Union, the National Miners Union, and the Needle Trades Workers Industrial Union (1928)—all three were thick in strikes (1928–31). As W(C)P delegate to the sixth Comintern congress, he was elected to the Executive Committee of the Communist International and appointed to its presidium (1928). He led the TUEL in founding the (first) Auto Workers Union and the Cannery and Agricultural Workers Industrial Union (1929). Via the W(C)P he went into the CPUSA, and was elected to its central committee, political committee, and secretariat (1929). He was secretary of the CPUSA's trade union department (1929–34) and founded the TUUL to organize the unorganized into industrial unions. He took the TUUL into the RILU and was appointed TUUL general secretary (1929–35).

Foster was elected (and reelected) CPUSA national chair (1930–44). He led the one-hundred-thousand-strong "unlawful assembly" against unemployment in New York's Union Square, for which he served six months in prisons on Blackwell's Island and Hart Island (1930). He led the foundation of the National Unemployment Council (1930) and led the National Hunger Marches (1931–32). He was elected to the Comintern's executive committee's presidium (1931). Foster was the CPUSA candidate for president in 1932, but suffered a heart attack and stroke, from which he had to convalesce until 1935. Although he never fully recovered, Foster remained active: he was CPUSA delegate to the seventh Comintern congress and was elected to the Comintern's executive committee and its presidium (1935). Within the party, he led the left opposition to the general secretary's leadership on the Popular Front (1935–39). He led the party in demanding US neutrality in European war (1939–41) but opposed the general secretary's ban on strikes during World War II, (1941–45). He opposed the CPUSA's self-dissolution into the Communist Political Association (1944–45), won the liquidation of the CPA and the restoration of the CPUSA, and was reelected its national chair (1945–57). Indicted under the Smith Act for sedition (1949), he was removed from trial for medical reasons (and remained under indictment the rest of his life); he defended the convicted in deposition and the public press.

Foster was the author of many works, including: (with Earl C. Ford) *Syndicalism* (1912); *The Great Steel Strike and Its Lessons* (1920); *The Railroaders' Next Step—Amalgamation* (1921); *The Russian Revolution* (1921); *The Revolutionary Crisis of 1918–1921, in Germany, England, Italy, and France* (1921); *Organize the Unorganized* (1926); *Strike Strategy* (1926); *Misleaders of Labor* (1927); *Toward Soviet America* (1932); *From Bryan to Stalin* (1937); *Manual of Industrial*

Unionism: Organizational Structure and Policies (1937);
Pages from a Worker's Life (1939); *Capitalism, Socialism,
and the War* (1940); *The War and Trade Unions* (1942);
Problems of Organized Labor Today (1946); *American
Trade Unionism, Principles and Organization, Strategy
and Tactics* (1947); *The New Europe* (1947); *Danger Ahead
for Organized Labor* (1948); *The Negro People in American
History* (1954); *History of the Communist Party of the
United States* (1952); *History of the Three Internationals*
(1955); and several other books and many more pamphlets.
After suffering further strokes in 1957 and 1959, William Z.
Foster died in Moscow in 1961 and was buried in Chicago.

Wyndham Mortimer was born in Karthaus, Pennsylvania
(1884), the son of a coal miner in the Knights of Labor.
He quit school at twelve to work in the mines and joined
the United Mine Workers (1900) and the SPA (1908). He
worked in Lorain, Ohio, steel mills; Pennsylvania and New
York Central railroads; and Cleveland, Ohio, streetcars. He
joined the IWW and was a drill operator in the White Motor
machine shops in Cleveland, where he learned technically
strategic positions (1917–36). Mortimer joined the CPUSA
(1932), unionized the White Motor workers, and affiliated
their local with the CPUSA-led Auto Workers Union (1933).
For cover, he led the local's conversion to a Federal Local
affiliated with the AFL. He was elected president of the
Cleveland Auto Council (1934) and vice president of the
United Auto Workers (UAW) in 1936 and played a central
role in organizing the UAW's industrially strategic strike
at the General Motors complex in Flint, Michigan, which
blew into the "Great GM Sit-Down Strike" (1936–37), crucial
to establishing the UAW in the US auto industry. Mortimer
was expelled from the UAW but then readmitted in 1938.
In coalition with the Reuther brothers, he moved the UAW
into the new CIO in 1938. He headed the UAW's organizing

in the West Coast aircraft industry (1939–41), unionized Vultee Aircraft, struck North American, and after refusing UAW orders to end strike, was fired by the UAW (1941). Mortimer served as an organizer for national CIO (1941–42). He resigned to work for Los Angeles unions and retired in 1945 to speak and write on labor. Mortimer died in Los Angeles in 1966. His memoir, *Organize! My Life as a Union Man*, was published in 1971.

Luca Perrone, born in Milan (1945), graduated from Università Cattolica-del Sacre Cuore in Milan (1968); conducted research in information, operations, systems, and industrial relations at the Pirelli Institute in Milan (1969–71); was Harkness Fellow-Research Associate in Sociology at UC-Berkeley (1971–74); professor of sociology, Università della Calabria (1974–77); and professor of political sciences, Università Estatale di Milano (1978–80). He died in a diving accident (1980).

Perrone's publications include: (with Erik O. Wright) "Marxist Class Categories and Income Inequality," *American Sociological Review* 42, no. 1 (February 1977): 32–55; "Positional Power and Propensity to Strike," ed. Erik O. Wright, *Politics and Society* 12, no. 2 (February 1983): 231–61; and "Positional Power, Strikes and Wages," ed. Erik O. Wright, *American Sociological Review* 49, no. 3 (June 1984): 413–21.

Notes

Introduction

1   Peter Olney, "The Arithmetic of Decline and Some Proposals for Renewal," *New Labor Forum* no. 10 (Spring–Summer 2002): 35–44.

2   Katherine Sciacchitano, "How Home Care Workers Came Out of the Shadows," *Dissent Magazine*, Winter 2014, https://www.dissentmagazine.org/article/how-home-care-workers-came-out-of-the-shadows; Jennifer Klein, "New Haven Rising," *Dissent Magazine* 62, no. 1 (Winter 2015): 45–54, https://www.dissentmagazine.org/article/new-haven-rising; and Eleni Schirmer, "Jane McAlevey's Vision for the Future of American Labor," *New Yorker*, June 10, 2020, https://www.newyorker.com/books/under-review/jane-mcaleveys-vision-for-the-future-of-american-labor.

3   Harvey Schwartz, *The March Inland: Origins of the ILWU Warehouse Division, 1934–1938* (San Francisco: ILWU, 2000). Originally published in 1978 by the Institute of Industrial Relations at UCLA.

4   John Womack Jr., *Zapata and the Mexican Revolution* (New York: Vintage, 1969).

5   John Womack Jr., "Working Power over Production: Labor History, Industrial Work, Economics, Sociology, and Strategic Position," XIV International Economic History Congress, Helsinki, June 2, 2006, Scribd, https://www.scribd.com/document/91807572/Womack-Working-Power-Over-Production.

6   John Womack Jr., *Posición estratégica y fuerza obrera: Hacia una nueva historia de los movimientos obreros* (Mexico City: El Fondo de Cultura Economica, 2007).

7   "Salting" is a labor tactic that involves a union member joining
         a nonunionized organization as an employee for the purpose of
         organizing a union there.

Situating Womack

1   Fernand Braudel, *The Perspective of the World*, vol. 3 of *Civilization
         and Capitalism, 15th to 18th Centuries* (New York: HarperCollins,
         1984).

2   Wyndham Mortimer, *Organize* (Boston: Beacon, 1971); Sidney
         Fine, *Sitdown: The General Motors Strike of 1936–1937* (Ann Arbor:
         University of Michigan Press, 2020). The best general overview of
         the 1920s and 1930s remains Irving Bernstein, *The Lean Years: A
         History of the American Worker, 1920–1933* (Baltimore: Penguin,
         1966); and *The Turbulent Years: A History of the American Worker,
         1933–1941* (Boston: Houghton Mifflin, 1971). See also Nelson
         Lichtenstein, *Reuther: The Most Dangerous Man in Detroit* (Urbana:
         University of Illinois Press, 1997); and Mike Davis, *Prisoners of the
         American Dream* (London: Verso, 1986).

3   Edward Lasker, *Chess Strategy* (London: G. Bell & Sons, 1921).

4   Raising theory to the level of practice: always, ultimately, testing
         theory (and historical investigations) in the proving ground of
         practical activity. Betsy Taylor and Herbert Reid, *Recovering the
         Commons: Democracy, Place and Social Justice* (Urbana: University
         of Illinois Press, 2010), with the idea of participatory reason; John
         Dewey, *Democracy and Education* (1916); Paulo Freire, *Pedagogy
         of the Oppressed* (New York: Herder and Herder, 1970); Myles
         Horton, *The Long Haul* (New York: Doubleday, 1990); here, the
         experience of A.J. Muste and the Brookwood Labor College in the
         1920s–1930s—and its relationship to the growth of the CIO gener-
         ation—is worthy of serious study.

5   Workers' sense of efficacy as unionists or future unionists, their
         collective organizational self-confidence, often stems from prac-
         tical knowledge in the work process itself. Developing the habit of
         generalizing from one's own experience comes from exposure to
         alternative experiences, which is one reason multicraft organizing
         and pedagogy are important.

6   Dale Carnegie, *How to Win Friends and Influence People* (New
         York: Simon and Schuster, 1936). I am not the only student of
         organizational practice who sees sincere mastery of Carnegie's
         interpersonal basics—essentially a practical expression of the
         idea of narrative imagination—as the golden key to organizational
         efficiency. Is this anything other than a practical knowledge
         expression of the difficult-to-teach quality that the best historians

and ethnographers also have—the capacity to see through the eyes of another? To engage with sincerity in the world from the other's point of view?

7   I tell the story from a North American point of view, based on my own experience, recognizing full well that the patterns are global.

8   In the 1980s, I held a journeyman's card in the Chicago Typographical Union, Local 16. With its continuous organizational existence dating back to the 1850s, the International Typographical Union was one of the proudest, oldest, and most democratic labor organizations in American history. But the new technology was making us redundant, and the union was shedding members rapidly. Merging with another union was the only way to preserve the last vestiges of power that had been eroded by the new machines. Gompers's Cigar Makers and Trumka's Mine Workers suffered similar fates.

9   Rand Wilson and Peter Olney, "The Message from the Amazon Union Defeat in Alabama Is Clear: Keep Organizing," *In These Times*, April 9, 2021, https://inthesetimes.com/article/amazon-union-defeat-alabama-bessemer-rwdsu-pro-act.

10 Glenn Perušek, "Class, Race and Political Strategy in the Rust Belt," Stansbury Forum, May 2017, https://stansburyforum.com/2017/05/30/class-race-and-political-strategy-in-the-rust-belt. The erosion of membership and dynamism to the US labor movement was already recognized even during its (relative) heyday. A young Martin Luther King Jr. could offer labor a vision of unity between the union movement's numbers and the civil rights movement's dynamism. See "Address at the Illinois State Convention of the American Federation of Labor and Congress of Industrial Organizations," October 7, 1965, http://okra.stanford.edu/en/permalink/document651007-002.

11 Tom Juravich and Kate Bronfenbrenner, *Ravenswood: The Steelworkers' Victory and the Revival of American Labor* (Ithaca, NY: ILR Press, 1999).

12 The history of the development of the comprehensive campaigns model has not been written. Stephen Lerner, "Let's Get Moving: Labor's Survival Depends on Organizing Industry-Wide for Justice and Power"; Andy Banks, "The Power and Promise of Community Unionism"; Joe Crump, "The Pressure Is On: Organizing with – out the NLRB"; Jack Metzgar, "Committed to Organizing: An Interview with Richard Bensinger," all in *Labor Research Review* 1, no. 18 (Fall/Winter 1991): 1–91; Stephen Lerner, "Three Steps to Reorganizing and Rebuilding the Labor Movement," *Labor Notes*, December 1, 2002, https://labornotes.org/2002/12/

three-steps-reorganizing-and-rebuilding-labor-movement-build-
ing-new-strength-and-unity-all (and responses); Juravich and
Bronfenbrenner, Ravenswood; Kate Bronfenbrenner, ed., *Global
Unions: Challenging Transnational Capital through Cross-Border
Campaigns* (Ithaca, NY: Cornell University Press, 2007); Kate
Bronfenbrenner and Robert Hickey, *Blueprint for Change: A
National Assessment of Winning Union Organizing Strategies*
(Ithaca, NY: Cornell Office of Labor Education Research, 2003);
Stephen Lerner, "An Immodest Proposal: A New Architecture for the
House of Labor," *New Labor Forum* 12, no. 2 (Summer 2003): 9–30;
Stephen Lerner, "Global Unions: A Solution to Labor's Worldwide
Decline," *New Labor Forum* 16, no. 1 (Winter 2007): 22–37; Rich
Yeselson, "Fortress Unionism," *Democracy*, Summer 2013, http://
democracyjournal. org/magazine/29/fortress-unionism; Peter
Olney, "Beyond the Waterfront," *Stansbury Forum*, August 26, 2019,
https://stansburyforum.com/2019/08/26/beyond-the-waterfront;
Peter Olney, "The Arithmetic of Decline and Some Proposals for
Renewal," *New Labor Forum* no. 10 (Spring–Summer 2002): 6–18;
Andrew Banks and John Russo, "The Development of International
Campaign – Based Network Structures: A Case Study of the IBT
and ITF World Council of UPS Unions," *Comparative Labor Law &
Policy Journal* 20 (1999): 543–68.

13   From this voluminous literature, some peaks: Sun Tzu, *The Art
of War*, trans. Samuel B. Griffith (London: Oxford University
Press, 1963); Thucydides, in both the Hobbes and the Landmark
editions; B.H. Liddell Hart, *Strategy*, 2nd rev. ed. (New York: Praeger,
1967). (An important contrary perspective on Liddell Hart is John
Mearsheimer, *Liddell Hart and the Weight of History* (Ithaca, NY:
Cornell University Press, 1988).)

I myself often think and teach in terms of military and sports
metaphors. American football is particularly useful, since I share
a familiarity with the game with many organizers; and it lends
itself well to the idea of broadening campaigns from direct ground
organizing to a multiform "modern" system of ground and air—
direct and indirect means of approach. Metaphors from music (the
orchestration of a symphony), cuisine (the planning and delivery
of a seven-course meal), or other fields are also appropriate and
should be developed.

The essence of strategic campaigning is thorough preparatory
research to plan campaigns that take on an opponent's strategy or
their alliances (and that simultaneously build out one's own alliances—as well as mobilizing latent internal resources). Strategic
objectives should be cast as defensive; tactics, on the other hand,

should be bold—with an emphasis on the unexpected. This is Periklean strategy as outlined by Thucydides, entirely in accord with both Sun Tzu and Liddell Hart's reading of a whole line of successful generals.

14　The worldview expressed in E.P. Thompson's *The Making of the English Working Class* (New York: Vintage, 1966) is the normative foundation for many on the labor Left. Any particular, historically situated working class has to make itself—through its institutions, aspirations, cultural practices. The idea of "self-creation" of a collective democratic subject, itself a cultural whole that is contingent on the actions, conflicts, and compromises that this necessitates. On research programs, see Imre Lakatos, *The Methodology of Scientific Research Programmes* (Cambridge: Cambridge University Press, 1978); Joseph Rouse, *Knowledge and Power: Toward a Political Philosophy of Science* (Ithaca, NY: Cornell University Press, 1987); Glenn Perušek, "Two Methodological Traditions in the Social Sciences," in *Shifting Terrain: Essays on Politics, History and Society* (New York: Peter Lang, 2006), 157–77.

15　Aristotle, *Politics*, 1253b34; Homer, *Iliad*, 18.369.

16　John Maynard Keynes, "Economic Possibilities for Our Grandchildren" (1930), in *Essays in Persuasion* (New York: Norton, 1963), 358–73, http://www.econ.yale.edu/smith/econ116a/keynes1.pdf. See especially Martin Ford, *The Lights in the Tunnel: Automation, Accelerating Technology and the Economy of the Future* (Wayne, PA: Acculant Publishing, 2009); and *The Rise of the Robots: Technology and the Threat of a Jobless Future* (New York: Basic Books, 2015); and the solid work of MIT's Erik Brynjolfsson and Andrew McAfee, *Race against the Machine: How the Digital Revolution Is Accelerating Innovation, Driving Productivity, and Irreversibly Transforming Employment and the Economy* (Lexington, MA: Digital Frontier Press, 2011); and *The Second Machine Age: Work, Progress, and Prosperity in a Time of Brilliant Technologies* (New York: Norton, 2014). Glenn Perušek, "Cleveland: City of Tomorrow?" *Belt Magazine*, March 23, 2015, https://beltmag.com/cleveland-city-of-tomorrow.

The "Foundry Interviews"

1　John T. Dunlop, *Industrial Relations Systems* (New York: Holt, 1958). See Selected Historical Biographies, 155–56.

2　Eugene Victor Debs (1855–1926), see Selected Historical Biographies, 154.

3　Jamie Dimon, chairman and CEO of JPMorgan Chase (the biggest bank in the United States), paid $29.5 million in 2017, net worth

$1.3 billion. Lloyd C. Blankfein, chairman and CEO of Goldman Sachs (fourth biggest bank in United States), paid $24 million in 2017, net worth $1.3 billion. (Both donate mainly to Democratic candidates.)

4   The Second International, aka the Socialist International, was founded in Paris 1889, a quasi-Marxist confederation of socialist and labor parties organized to win elections for socialism. The most important parties were in the German empire, France, Great Britain, Belgium, Netherlands, with others in Austrian and Russian empires, Italy, Switzerland, the United States, and elsewhere. The Second International failed in 1914 to oppose World War I, when German and French parliamentary parties voted for national budgets for the war. The Third International, aka the Communist International, or Comintern, was founded in Moscow in 1919, a centralized multinational alliance (Lenin's Russian word was *soyuz*, as in "union," "league," or "alliance") of Communist, revolutionary socialist, syndicalist, and workers' parties, as Comintern "sections," for proletarians worldwide aiming to overthrow international capitalism and to construct socialism worldwide. The dominant section was the Communist Party of the Soviet Union, with others of importance in Germany, France, Britain, and the United States. Substantial sections also existed in China, Dutch East Indies (present-day Indonesia), British Union of South Africa, Argentina, Brazil, and Mexico. The Second International dissolved in 1943.

5   Wyndham Mortimer (1884–1966), see Selected Historical Biographies, 165–66.

6   William Edward Foster (1881–1961), see Selected Historical Biographies, 161–65.

7   For more information about Farrell Dobbs (1907–1983) and the four Dunne brothers, see Selected Historical Biographies, 156–61.

8   Erik Olin Wright (1947–2019) studied at Harvard and Balliol, receiving a PhD from the University of California, Berkeley, in sociology, in 1976. He became a professor of sociology, University of Wisconsin–Madison, in 1976, with special interests in social stratification and analytical Marxism. He is the author of *Class, Crisis, and the State* (London: NLB, 1978); *Class Structure and Income Determination* (New York: Academic Press, 1979); *Classes* (London: Verso, 1985); *Class Counts: Comparative Studies in Class Analysis* (Cambridge: Cambridge University Press, 1997); *Envisioning Real Utopias* (London: Verso, 2010); and *Understanding Class* (London: Verso, 2015), as well as many other books and scholarly articles.

9   Luca Perrone (1945–1980), see Selected Historical Biographies, 166.

10   A.A. Belyk, "A Note on the Origins of Input-Output Analysis and the Contributions of the Early Soviet Economists: Chayanov, Bogdanov and Kritsman," *Soviet Studies* 41, no. 3 (July 1989): 426–29; Wassily Leontief, *The Structure of the American Economy, 1919–1929* (Cambridge, MA: Harvard University, 1941); Belyk, *Input-Output Economics* (New York: Oxford University, 1966). Leontief won the Nobel Prize in Economics in 1973.

11   Richard J. Campbell, "The Smart Grid: Status and Outlook," Congressional Research Service, 7-5700, April 10, 2018, https://sgp.fas.org/crs/misc/R45156.pdf.

12   John Pencavel, born in London (1943), studied at the University of London and received a PhD in Economics from Princeton (1969). He has been a professor of economics at Stanford University since 1969, with his main research in labor economics. He is the author of *Labor Markets under Trade Unionism: Employment, Wages, and Hours* (Oxford: Blackwell, 1991) among other books and scholarly articles in economics.

13   "Word for Word/A Fire Captain's Eulogy," *New York Times*, December 23, 2001, https://www.nytimes.com/2001/12/23/weekinreview/word-for-word-fire-captain-s-eulogy-first-last-unbreakable-links-chain-command.html.

14   Ford's River Rouge auto complex in Dearborn, Michigan, was constructed during 1917–1928. Measuring 1.5 by 1 mile, it consisted of ninety-three buildings, with 360 acres of factory floor. It had its own docks (on the River Rouge), railroad, power plant, and steel mill. At the time, it was the largest integrated manufacturing system in the world, the model of "vertical integration," producing Ford vehicle parts and cars, trucks, and tractors. At one time, the Rouge complex employed more than one hundred thousand workers. Today there are still six thousand workers at Ford's Rouge facilities, and steel is still made there by AK Steel.

Should Spartacus Have Organized the Roman Citizenry Rather Than the Slaves?

1   See Robert Bussell, *Fighting for Total Person Unionism: Harold Gibbons, Ernest Calloway and Working-Class Citizenship* (Champaign: University of Illinois Press, 2015).

Relaying These Insights Is More Urgent Now Than Ever

1   For a good overview of the differences between these two paths, see Frank Bardacke, *Trampling Out the Vintage: Cesar Chavez and the Two Souls of the United Farm Workers* (London: Verso, 2012).

2   Kim Moody, interviewed by Chris Brooks, "Labor's New Sources of Leverage," *Labor Notes*, August 12, 2016, https://www.labornotes.org/moodyinterview.

No Magic Bullet: Technically Strategic Power Alone Is Not Enough

1   Erik Olin Wright, "Working-Class Power, Capitalist-Class Interests, and Class Compromise," *American Journal of Sociology* 105, no. 4 (January 2000): 957–1002.

2   For an empirically grounded case study illustrating this argument, see Katy Fox-Hodess and Camilo Santibáñez Rebolledo, "The Social Foundations of Structural Power: Strategic Position, Worker Unity and External Alliances in the Making of the Chilean Dockworkers Movement," *Global Labour Journal* 11, no. 3 (2020): 222–38. This article is available through open access at the *Global Labour Journal* website: https://mulpress.mcmaster.ca/globallabour/article/view/4236.

3   Katy Fox-Hodess, "Worker Power, Trade Union Strategy, and International Connections: Dockworker Unionism in Colombia and Chile," *Latin American Politics and Society* 61, no. 3 (August 2019): 29–54.

4   Katy Fox-Hodess, "(Re-)Locating the Local and National in the Global: Multi-scalar Political Alignment in Transnational European Dockworker Union Campaigns." *British Journal of Industrial Relations* 55, no. 3 (September 2017): 626–47.

Organizing Strategic Workers on "the Seam"

1   The UAW's 2019 strike at GM and subsequent concessionary agreements at Ford and Chrysler leap to mind.

2   The two longshore unions are very different in their political orientation, yet in recent decades they have both failed to shake off the limitations of craft unionism in order to wield their great economic power to transform conditions for workers further down the supply chain in trucking, warehousing, and retail. Most concerning is the craft unionism of the ILWU, where Longshore Division leadership has singularly focused on the waterfront terminal. They have ignored the fate of all other workers in the maritime supply chain. The Pacific Maritime Association (an employer group) has perfected the art of ensnarling the ILWU in defensive fights over jurisdiction and contract violations, removing resources that would be used for organizing and research in any strategic vision of maritime cargo supply chains. That the ILWU has wandered far from its founding mission to organize

industrially should be of deep concern to all revolutionary socialists, as it is one of the last of the truly left-wing unions on or near
a Womackian seam.

3   The American railroad is similarly thoroughly unionized. Whereas
the craft unionism of the ILWU has to do with its relation to the
rest of the transportation industry, railroad workers are even
more fractured and dispersed. Rail labor consists of twelve unions,
some of which belong to the same international, but all of which
act autonomously. This has been a recipe for disaster, particularly
in recent years as rail labor has completely failed to take economic
advantage of the record profitability of the monopolistic Class 1
Railroads. None of the rail unions show any signs of being aware
of their awesome power to propel organizing in the supply chains
where their members toil.

4   Being "organized" involves workers making the most of their
structural *and* associational power. I emphatically agree with
Womack that for change to stick, material power must be brought
to the equation by workers on the seam. But my experience as an
organizer in the ILWU and with the BMWED (rail) has led me to
believe that structural and associational power need to be wielded
dialectically for workers to achieve the maximum degree of their
transformational potential.

5   Vital Womackian seams are everywhere and ripe for the pick-
ing by thoughtful organizers aided by researchers and visionary,
courageous working-class leaders. For example, the maritime
cargo unloaded at West Coast ports is railed into the North
American interior where the Teamsters Union has had great
success winning first contracts at "intermodal yards" in Chicago
(the most vital rail hub in the US) and the Inland Empire east
of Los Angeles. In the most recent case at the Norfolk Southern
intermodal yard in May 2020, a "practice picket" threatening a
full-blown strike brought the boss back to the table and resulted
in an agreement within days. These yards—and the maritime cargo
they process—are so sensitive that any disruption leads to greatly
multiplied disruptions both up and down the supply chain.

   These seams, however, appear and vanish with relative speed
requiring ongoing vigilance to meet the revolutionary nature of
capitalist production. As the organized sections of the working
class, we can never rest in our work on the Womackian seams. The
capitalists—with all their resources—certainly never do.

6   See Howard Kimeldorf's excellent *Reds or Rackets* (Berkeley:
University of California Press, 1988).

Who Will Lead the Campaign?

1   Harry Braverman. *Labor and Monopoly Capital: The Degradation of Work in the Twentieth Century* (New York: Monthly Review Press, 1974).

2   Bryan D. Palmer, "Before Braverman: Harry Frankel and the American Workers' Movement," *Monthly Review* 50, no. 8 (January 1999): 33–46.

Abandon the Banking Method!

1   The banking concept of education is one in which "knowledge is a gift bestowed by those who consider themselves knowledgeable upon those whom they consider to know nothing." "Education thus becomes an act of depositing, in which the students are the depositories and the teacher is the depositor." Paulo Freire, *Pedagogy of the Oppressed* (New York: Herder and Herder, 1970), 72.

2   Tara Fenwick, "Tightrope Walkers and Solidarity Sisters: Critical Workplace Educators in the Garment Industry," *International Journal of Lifelong Education* 26, no. 3 (May 2007): 315–28.

3   Linda Delp, Miranda Outman-Kramer, Susan J. Schurman, and Kent Wong, eds., *Teaching for Change: Popular Education and the Labor Movement* (Los Angeles: UCLA Center for Labor Research and Education, 2002).

4   Transformative learning is the process of effecting change in a frame of reference. Adults have acquired a coherent body of experience—associations, concepts, values, feelings, conditioned responses—frames of reference that define their life world. Frames of reference are the structures of assumptions through which we understand our experiences. They selectively shape and delimit expectations, perceptions, cognition, and feelings. They set our "line of action." Once set, we automatically move from one specific mental or behavioral activity to another. We have a strong tendency to reject ideas that fail to fit our preconceptions, labeling those ideas as unworthy of consideration—aberrations, nonsense, irrelevant, weird, or mistaken. When circumstances permit, transformative learners move toward a frame of reference that is more inclusive, discriminating, self-reflective, and integrative of experience. Jack Mezirow, "Transformative Learning: Theory to Practice," *New Directions for Adult and Continuing Education* 74 (Summer 1997): 5–12.

Epilogue? No, An Update and Directions

1   U.S. Bureau of Labor Statistics, *Occupational Outlook Handbook*, https://www.bls.gov/ooh/a-z-index.htm.

2   R.H. Coase, "The Nature of the Firm," *Economica* 4, no. 16 (November 1937): 386–405; Ronald H. Coase, "Prize Lecture: The Institutional Structure of Production," https://www.nobelprize.org/prizes/economic-sciences/1991/coase/facts.

About the Authors

John Womack Jr., is the Robert Woods Bliss Professor of Latin American History and Economics, emeritus, at Harvard University. He served as chairman of the Department of History, 1982–85, and acting chairman, 1991–92. Born and raised in Norman, Oklahoma, he first joined a union, the International Laborers and Hod Carriers, while in high school, earning a union wage in summer construction work. He held his card until he graduated from college and went to work at the *Louisville Times*—then into graduate studies and later into academic work. His publications include *Zapata and the Mexican Revolution* (1968) and *Rebellion in Chiapas: An Historical Reader* (1999).

★

Gene Bruskin has been active for forty years in the labor movement as local union president, organizer, and campaign coordinator for local and national unions. From 1992 to 1994 he served as Labor Deputy for Jesse Jackson (National Rainbow Coalition). He was secretary-treasurer for the Food and Allied Services (AFL-CIO) from 1996 to 2005. He was the UFCW campaign director for the Justice@ Smithfield campaign in North Carolina, 2006–8, and established the Strategic Campaigns Department for the American Federation of Teachers, 2009–12. Gene cofounded US Labor Against the War and has been active in other international labor solidarity efforts. Since retirement he consults for union organizing programs and has written and produced two musicals for and about workers.

Since 2015, **Carey Dall** has coordinated the Internal Organizing Department of the Brotherhood of Maintenance of Way (BMWED-IBT), which represents track and structure maintenance workers on the major railroads throughout the lower forty-eight states. Previously Dall was a fifteen-year member of the International Longshore and Warehouse Union (ILWU), where he spent six years as an international organizer. He got his start in the labor movement as a salt working with the ILWU to organize bike and driver messengers in the Bay Area.

Dan DiMaggio is an assistant editor at *Labor Notes*, where he covers workers in telecommunications, airlines, and the building trades. He first became active in the labor movement as a student activist in the Harvard Living Wage Campaign of the early 2000s. He holds master's degrees in Latin American labor history from Tufts University and sociology from New York University. His writings have been published in *New Labor Forum* and *Monthly Review*. He is forever appreciative of the grounding in historical materialism that he obtained through several Latin American history courses with Professor Womack as an undergraduate at Harvard.

Bill Fletcher Jr. is executive editor of globalafricanworker. com, past president of TransAfrica Forum, and a longtime trade unionist and writer. He is the coauthor (with Fernando Gapasin) of *Solidarity Divided*; author of *"They're*

Bankrupting Us" and *Twenty Other Myths about Unions,* and the mystery novel *The Man Who Fell from the Sky.*

Robert Gumpert, a California-based photographer with extensive international experience documenting social issues and institutions, including service and industrial work, jails and the criminal justice system, and emergency rooms and paramedics. His collaborative *Take A Picture/Tell a Story* project in the San Francisco County jails. exchanges inmates' portraits for their stories. He has also created abstract art from the textures and colors of the bridges, walls, highway supports, and fallen leaves of London and San Francisco.

Robert's new book, *Division Street*, is published by Dewi Lewis Publishing and can be ordered at https://www. dewilewis.com/.

Katy Fox-Hodess is a lecturer in Work, Employment, People and Organisations at the University of Sheffield. Her research focuses on class formation and labor internationalism among dockworkers. Katy worked as an organizer with the ILWU in California prior to receiving her PhD.

Jane McAlevey is an organizer and author. After twenty-five years in the field, she began writing about how to win hard organizing campaigns. She is currently a senior policy fellow at the University of California at Berkeley's Labor Center and the strike correspondent for *The Nation* magazine. She leads a global organizing training program through the Rosa Luxemburg Stiftung, which has brought together over twenty-five thousand workers from 110 countries since 2020.

Jack Metzgar is emeritus professor of humanities at Roosevelt University in Chicago, founding editor of

Labor Research Review, and director of Roosevelt's Labor Leadership Program. His experience as a labor educator includes teaching for AFSCME, the AFL-CIO's Meany Center, and the Labor Center at the University of Massachusetts–Amherst. He is the author of *Bridging the Divide: Working-Class Culture in a Middle-Class Society* and *Striking Steel: Solidarity Remembered*. A founder and past president of the Working-Class Studies Association, he is a regular contributor to the *Working-Class Perspectives* blog.

Joel Ochoa is the son of a railroad worker and originally from Chiapas, Mexico. As a high school student he participated in the 1968 student movement in Mexico City. In 1970 he began participating in a national movement for popular education and helped to create independent high schools in several cities, including the Preparatoria Popular Tacuba in Mexico, City. In 1973, as a student at the National Autonomous University of Mexico's School of Philosophy and Letters, he was singled out by the government of then president Luis Echeverría and forced to leave the country. In the US, Ochoa joined an organization of immigrant workers and their families named CASA-HGT, founded by the legendary Bert Corona, and became an active labor and community organizer. In 1988 he was hired to work for the newly created associate membership program of the AFL-CIO California Immigrant Workers Association and participated in some of the most significant organizing campaigns in Southern California during the late 1980s and early 1990s. He became an international representative of the IAMAW and represented the union in thirteen western states, including Hawaii and Alaska. Ochoa is currently retired and residing in Southern California.

Peter Olney is a retired director of organizing for the International Longshore and Warehouse Union. He was associate director of the University of California's Institute for Labor and Employment. Olney holds a master's in business administration from UCLA. He resides in San Francisco and teaches building trades union organizers as a member of the faculty of the Building Trades Academy at Michigan State University. Olney is an editor of *The Stansbury Forum* (stansburyforum.com). Contact olneyrom@gmail.com.

Glenn Perušek conducts strategic research for organizing and contract campaigns and is a member of the faculty of the Building Trades Academy at Michigan State University. He directed the Center for Strategic Research at the national AFL-CIO and worked in strategic research and campaigns at the IBEW and the International Brotherhood of Teamsters. His work includes *Tragedy and Necessity: From Sarajevo to the Berlin Wall* (forthcoming), *Shifting Terrain*; *Depth of Field* (on filmmaker Stanley Kubrick), and *Trade Union Politics: American Unions and Economic Change*. Glenn earned a BA summa cum laude from Kent State University. He holds a PhD from the University of Chicago, where he was Merriam Fellow and winner of the Baker Prize, a research competition in the social sciences. Glenn was a journeyman member of the Chicago Typographical Union. Contact gperusek@gmail.com.

Melissa Shetler works with Climate Jobs National Resource Center and Cornell's Labor Leading on Climate Initiative as a labor and workforce consultant. She is a cofounder and former executive director of Pathways to Apprenticeship, a preapprenticeship program that assists historically marginalized communities gain access to union construction careers. She worked as a community organizer and member education facilitator with the Laborers Eastern Region Organizing Fund and became the director of organizing, and later political director, for the Metallic Lathers and Reinforcing Ironworkers Local 46 (NY). Melissa earned her BA from SUNY Empire State College, where she continues to facilitate classes in theater for social change and has a master's degree in adult learning and leadership from Teachers College. She is also a jazz vocalist and recently welcomed twins into the world.

Rand Wilson has extensive experience as a union organizer and labor communicator. Originally a member of the Oil, Chemical and Atomic Workers Union in Boston, Wilson went on staff as an organizer with Communications Workers of America and several other unions. In 1991, he was the founding director of Massachusetts Jobs with Justice. Hired by the International Brotherhood of Teamsters in 1995, he worked as communications coordinator for the historic 1997 UPS contract campaign and strike. In 2016, he helped cofound Labor for Bernie and was elected a Sanders delegate to the Democratic National Convention. Since then, he has been an active member of Our Revolution. In 2020, he again volunteered with Labor for Bernie and was appointed to the DNC Credentials Committee. From 2011 until 2021, Wilson was an organizer and chief of staff at SEIU Local 888 in Boston. He is board chair for the ICA Group and the Fund for Jobs Worth Owning, a trustee for the Center for the Study of Public Policy and the Somerville Job Creation and Retention Trust, a member of the Somerville Ward Six Democratic Committee, and convener of Somerville Stands Together, a community-labor coalition.

Index

Page numbers in *italic* refer to illustrations. "Passim" (literally "scattered") indicates intermittent discussion of a topic over a cluster of pages.

ABOUT PM PRESS

PM Press is an independent, radical publisher of books and media to educate, entertain, and inspire. Founded in 2007 by a small group of people with decades of publishing, media, and organizing experience, PM Press amplifies the voices of radical authors, artists, and activists. Our aim is to deliver bold political ideas and vital stories to all walks of life and arm the dreamers to demand the impossible. We have sold millions of copies of our books, most often one at a time, face to face. We're old enough to know what we're doing and young enough to know what's at stake. Join us to create a better world.

PM Press
PO Box 23912
Oakland, CA 94623
www.pmpress.org

PM Press in Europe
europe@pmpress.org
www.pmpress.org.uk

FRIENDS OF PM PRESS

These are indisputably momentous times—the financial system is melting down globally and the Empire is stumbling. Now more than ever there is a vital need for radical ideas.

In the many years since its founding—and on a mere shoestring—PM Press has risen to the formidable challenge of publishing and distributing knowledge and entertainment for the struggles ahead. With hundreds of releases to date, we have published an impressive and stimulating array of literature, art, music, politics, and culture. Using every available medium, we've succeeded in connecting those hungry for ideas and information to those putting them into practice.

Friends of PM allows you to directly help impact, amplify, and revitalize the discourse and actions of radical writers, filmmakers, and artists. It provides us with a stable foundation from which we can build upon our early successes and provides a much-needed subsidy for the materials that can't necessarily pay their own way. You can help make that happen—and receive every new title automatically delivered to your door once a month—by joining as a Friend of PM Press. And, we'll throw in a free T-shirt when you sign up.

Here are your options:

- **$30 a month** Get all books and pamphlets plus 50% discount on all webstore purchases

- **$40 a month** Get all PM Press releases (including CDs and DVDs) plus 50% discount on all webstore purchases

- **$100 a month** Superstar—Everything plus PM merchandise, free downloads, and 50% discount on all webstore purchases

For those who can't afford $30 or more a month, we have **Sustainer Rates** at $15, $10 and $5. Sustainers get a free PM Press T-shirt and a 50% discount on all purchases from our website.

Your Visa or Mastercard will be billed once a month, until you tell us to stop. Or until our efforts succeed in bringing the revolution around. Or the financial meltdown of Capital makes plastic redundant. Whichever comes first.

Fighting Times: Organizing on the Front Lines of the Class War

Jon Melrod

ISBN: 978-1-62963-965-9
$24.95   320 pages

Deeply personal, astutely political, *Fighting Times: Organizing on the Front Lines of the Class War* recounts the thirteen-year journey of Jon Melrod to harness working-class militancy and jump start a revolution on the shop floor of American Motors. Melrod faces termination, dodges the FBI, outwits collaborators in the UAW, and becomes a central figure in a lawsuit against the rank-and-file newsletter *Fighting Times*, as he strives to build a class-conscious workers' movement from the bottom up.

A radical to the core, Melrod was a key part of campus insurrection at the University of Wisconsin, Madison. He left campus for the factory in 1972, hired along with hundreds of youthful job seekers onto the mind-numbing assembly line. *Fighting Times* paints a portrait of these rebellious and alienated young hires, many of whom were Black Vietnam vets.

Containing dozens of archival photographs, *Fighting Times* captures the journey of a militant antiracist revolutionary who rose to the highest elected ranks of his UAW local without compromising his politics or his dedication to building a class-conscious workers' movement. The book will arm and inspire a new generation of labor organizers with the skills and attitude to challenge the odds and fight the egregious abuses of the exploitative capitalist system.

"An eloquent voice from the frontlines of the hard, bitter, exhilarating struggles for freedom and justice that have made the world a better place, and an inspiring guide for carrying the crucial struggle forward."
—Noam Chomsky

"To organize communities and workers, you have to listen to them. Jon Melrod's many stories show he did just that—and had a blast, too, as they turned their creativity and solidarity against the boss. Yes, there's a lot to be learned from Melrod's tales, but they're also a joy to read."
—Ken Paff, cofounder of Teamsters for a Democratic Union

Labor Law for the Rank and Filer: Building Solidarity While Staying Clear of the Law (2nd Edition)

Staughton Lynd and Daniel Gross

ISBN: 978-1-60486-419-9
$12.00   120 pages

Have you ever felt your blood boil at work but lacked the tools to fight back and win? Or have you acted together with your co-workers, made progress, but wondered what to do next? If you are in a union, do you find that the union operates top-down just like the boss and ignores the will of its members?

Labor Law for the Rank and Filer: Building Solidarity While Staying Clear of the Law is a guerrilla legal handbook for workers in a precarious global economy. Blending cutting-edge legal strategies for winning justice at work with a theory of dramatic social change from below, Staughton Lynd and Daniel Gross deliver a practical guide for making work better while re-invigorating the labor movement.

Labor Law for the Rank and Filer demonstrates how a powerful model of organizing called "Solidarity Unionism" can help workers avoid the pitfalls of the legal system and utilize direct action to win. This new revised and expanded edition includes new cases governing fundamental labor rights as well as an added section on Practicing Solidarity Unionism. This new section includes chapters discussing the hard-hitting tactic of working to rule; organizing under the principle that no one is illegal; and building grassroots solidarity across borders to challenge neoliberalism, among several other new topics. Illustrative stories of workers' struggles make the legal principles come alive.

"Workers' rights are under attack on every front. Bosses break the law every day. For 30 years Labor Law for the Rank and Filer *has been arming workers with an introduction to their legal rights (and the limited means to enforce them) while reminding everyone that real power comes from workers' solidarity."*
—Alexis Buss, former General Secretary-Treasurer of the IWW

Solidarity Unionism: Rebuilding the Labor Movement from Below, Second Edition

Staughton Lynd with an Introduction by Immanuel Ness and illlustrations by Mike Konopacki

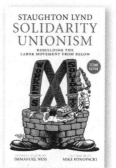

ISBN: 978-1-62963-096-0
$14.95   128 pages

Solidarity Unionism is critical reading for all who care about the future of labor. Drawing deeply on Staughton Lynd's experiences as a labor lawyer and activist in Youngstown, OH, and on his profound understanding of the history of the Congress of Industrial Organizations (CIO), *Solidarity Unionism* helps us begin to put not only movement but also vision back into the labor movement.

While many lament the decline of traditional unions, Lynd takes succor in the blossoming of rank-and-file worker organizations throughout the world that are countering rapacious capitalists and those comfortable labor leaders that think they know more about work and struggle than their own members. If we apply a new measure of workers' power that is deeply rooted in gatherings of workers and communities, the bleak and static perspective about the sorry state of labor today becomes bright and dynamic.

To secure the gains of solidarity unions, Staughton has proposed parallel bodies of workers who share the principles of rank-and-file solidarity and can coordinate the activities of local workers' assemblies. Detailed and inspiring examples include experiments in workers' self-organization across industries in steel-producing Youngstown, as well as horizontal networks of solidarity formed in a variety of U.S. cities and successful direct actions overseas.

This is a tradition that workers understand but labor leaders reject. After so many failures, it is time to frankly recognize that the century-old system of recognition of a single union as exclusive collective bargaining agent was fatally flawed from the beginning and doesn't work for most workers. If we are to live with dignity, we must collectively resist. This book is not a prescription but reveals the lived experience of working people continuously taking risks for the common good.

New Forms of Worker Organization: The Syndicalist and Autonomist Restoration of Class Struggle Unionism

Edited by Immanuel Ness
with a foreword by Staughton Lynd

ISBN: 978-1-60486-956-9
$24.95   336 pages

Bureaucratic labor unions are under assault. Most unions have surrendered the achievements of the mid-twentieth century, when the working class was a militant force for change throughout the world. Now trade unions seem incapable of defending, let alone advancing, workers' interests.

As unions implode and weaken, workers are independently forming their own unions, drawing on the tradition of syndicalism and autonomism—a resurgence of self-directed action that augurs a new period of class struggle throughout the world. In Africa, Asia, the Americas, and Europe, workers are rejecting leaders and forming authentic class-struggle unions rooted in sabotage, direct action, and striking to achieve concrete gains.

This is the first book to compile workers' struggles on a global basis, examining the formation and expansion of radical unions in the Global South and Global North. The tangible evidence marshaled in this book serves as a handbook for understanding the formidable obstacles and concrete opportunities for workers challenging neoliberal capitalism, even as the unions of the old decline and disappear.

Contributors include Au Loong-Yu, Bai Ruixue, Arup K. Sen, Shawn Hattingh, Piotr Bizyukov and Irina Olimpieva, Genese M. Sodikoff, Aviva Chomsky, Dario Bursztyn, Gabriel Kuhn, Erik Forman, Steven Manicastri, Arup Kumar Sen, and Jack Kirkpatrick.

Strike! 50th Anniversary Edition

Jeremy Brecher with a Preface by
Sara Nelson and a Foreword by Kim
Kelly

ISBN: 978-1-62963-800-3 (paperback)
      978-1-62963-856-0 (hardcover)
$28.95/$60.00   640 pages

Jeremy Brecher's *Strike!* narrates the dramatic
story of repeated, massive, and sometimes violent revolts by ordinary
working people in America. Involving nationwide general strikes, the
seizure of vast industrial establishments, nonviolent direct action
on a massive scale, and armed battles with artillery and tanks, this
exciting hidden history is told from the point of view of the rank-and-
file workers who lived it. Encompassing the repeated repression of
workers' rebellions by company-sponsored violence, local police, state
militias, and the US Army and National Guard, it reveals a dimension of
American history rarely found in the usual high school or college history
course.

Since its original publication in 1972, no book has done as much as
Strike! to bring US labor history to a wide audience. Now this fiftieth
anniversary edition brings the story up to date with chapters covering
the "mini-revolts of the 21st century," including Occupy Wall Street and
the Fight for Fifteen. The new edition contains over a hundred pages
of new materials and concludes by examining a wide range of current
struggles, ranging from #BlackLivesMatter, to the great wave of teachers
strikes "for the soul of public education," to the global "Student Strike for
Climate," that may be harbingers of mass strikes to come.

"*Jeremy Brecher's* Strike! *is a classic of American historical writing. This
new edition, bringing his account up to the present, comes amid rampant
inequality and growing popular resistance. No book could be more timely for
those seeking the roots of our current condition.*"
—Eric Foner, Pulitzer Prize winner and DeWitt Clinton Professor of
History at Columbia University

"*Magnificent—a vivid, muscular labor history, just updated and rereleased by
PM Press, which should be at the side of anyone who wants to understand
the deep structure of force and counterforce in America.*"
—JoAnn Wypijewski, author of *Killing Trayvons: An Anthology of American
Violence*

Working Class History: Everyday Acts of Resistance & Rebellion

Edited by Working Class History
with a Foreword by Noam Chomsky

ISBN: 978-1-62963-823-2 (paperback)
       978-1-62963-887-4 (hardcover)
$20.00/$59.95   352 pages

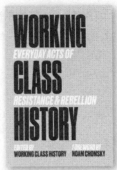

History is not made by kings, politicians, or a few rich individuals—it is made by all of us. From the temples of ancient Egypt to spacecraft orbiting Earth, workers and ordinary people everywhere have walked out, sat down, risen up, and fought back against exploitation, discrimination, colonization, and oppression.

Working Class History presents a distinct selection of people's history through hundreds of "on this day in history" anniversaries that are as diverse and international as the working class itself. Women, young people, people of color, workers, migrants, Indigenous people, LGBT+ people, disabled people, older people, the unemployed, home workers, and every other part of the working class have organized and taken action that has shaped our world, and improvements in living and working conditions have been won only by years of violent conflict and sacrifice. These everyday acts of resistance and rebellion highlight just some of those who have struggled for a better world and provide lessons and inspiration for those of us fighting in the present. Going day by day, this book paints a picture of how and why the world came to be as it is, how some have tried to change it, and the lengths to which the rich and powerful have gone to maintain and increase their wealth and influence.

This handbook of grassroots movements, curated by the popular Working Class History project, features many hidden histories and untold stories, reinforced with inspiring images, further reading, and a foreword from legendary author and dissident Noam Chomsky.

"I've learned so much from reading Working Class History. *It's a fountainhead of vital and inspiring information about the international class struggle. WCH is a crucial antidote to the twenty-first-century post-truth right-wing media blitz 24/7 assault on our senses. It's important to have revolutionary heroes and knowledge of past struggles to inspire the rebel souls of the future. Long may WCH inspire!"*
—Bobby Gillespie, lead singer of Primal Scream

WISDOM
FOR OUR
WORRIES

Also by Bill Crowder

Before Christmas

For This He Came

God of Surprise

Gospel on the Mountains

Let's Talk

Moving beyond Failure

My Hope Is in You

One Thing Is Necessary

Overcoming Life's Challenges

Seeing the Heart of Christ

The Spotlight of Faith

Trusting God in Hard Times

Windows on Christmas

Windows on Easter

Devotionals

A Compassionate Heart

A Present Peace